Latin America

Development and conflict since 1945

John Ward

London and New York

First published 1997
by Routledge
11 New Fetter Lane, London EC4P 4EE

Simultaneously published in the USA and Canada
by Routledge
29 West 35th Street, New York, NY 10001

Typeset in Times by Routledge
Printed and bound in Great Britain by Clays Ltd, St. Ives PLC

British Library Cataloguing in Publication Data
A catalogue record for this book is available from the British Library

Library of Congress Cataloguing in Publication Data
Ward, John, 1946–
Latin America: conflict and development since 1945 / John Ward. (The
making of the contemporary world)
Includes bibliographical references and index.
1. Latin America–Economic conditions–1945– 2. Latin
American–Foreign economic relations. 3. Latin America–Social
conditions.
I. Title. II. Series.
HC125.W37   1997   97-241
330.98′0033–dc21   CIP

ISBN 0–415–14725–5

Latin America

The Making of the Contemporary World
Edited by Eric Evans and Ruth Henig
University of Lancaster

The Making of the Contemporary World series provides challenging interpretations of contemporary issues and debates within strongly defined historical frameworks. The range of the series is global, with each volume drawing together material from a range of disciplines – including economics, politics and sociology. The books in this series present compact, indispensable introductions for students studying the modern world.

Forthcoming titles include:

Thatcher and Thatcherism
 Eric J Evans
The Soviet Union in World Politics, 1945-1991
 Geoffrey Roberts
The Uniting of Europe:
 From Discord to Concord
 Stanley Henig
International Economy since 1945
 Sidney Pollard
The United Nations in the Contemporary World
 David Whittaker
China Under Communism
 Alan Lawrance
The Cold War
 An interdisciplinary History
 David Painter
The Green Movement
 Dick Richardson
The Irish Question
 Patrick Maume
Decolonization
 Raymond Betts
Right Wing Extremism
 Paul Hainsworth

Contents

Illustrations

Acknowledgements

I am grateful to the series editors, their advisers, and the staff at Routledge, for commenting on drafts of this book. I should also like to thank my wife for her support during the process of composition.

Latin America, 1994 (population in millions; output per head, US $, purchasing power parities)

Source World Bank 1996: 188–9, 222

1 Introduction

Latin American history began in 1492 when Christopher Columbus, sponsored by the Spanish crown, led a naval expedition across the Atlantic and made landfall on various Caribbean islands. Further voyages of exploration and settlement followed. At first the newcomers concentrated their activities in the West Indies, working alluvial gold deposits and exterminating most of the indigenous inhabitants, who were used as forced labour. Then from 1519 Spanish adventurers reached the mainland, where they found and quickly subjugated large 'Indian'[1] populations, concentrated in Central America and the Andean highlands of South America. These regions would become the main centres of Spain's transatlantic empire, which by 1600 stretched 6,000 miles, from what is now the southwestern United States to central Chile and Argentina. For comparison, by 1750, after a century and a half of colonization, British settlers in North America had penetrated only about 200 miles inland from the eastern seaboard, along a 1,000 mile front. The Spanish conquistadors advanced so rapidly because of their eagerness to acquire the gold and silver which was available in great quantities, an aggressive military spirit, a wish to spread the Catholic Christian faith, and the weakness of the established indigenous empires (the Aztecs in Mexico, the Incas in Peru). The Spanish American economy came to be based on the extraction of tribute from the Indians, and the mining of precious metals. The colonial elite also established large agricultural estates (*haciendas*) to supply the mines, and the towns where most Spanish settlers, immigrant and locally born (creole), took up residence.

At first the Spanish comprised a small minority among the conquered Indians. However, the diseases introduced to the Americas by the Europeans devastated Indian populations, while there was a rapid growth in the number of whites and *mestizos* (people of mixed white/Indian descent). Also black slaves were imported from Africa.

By the early nineteenth century the population of Spanish America, totalling about 16 million, was made up roughly as follows: 18 per cent white, 28 per cent *mestizo* or mulatto (of mixed white/black race), 42 per cent Indian, and 12 per cent black (Skidmore and Smith 1997: 25).

The coastal zone of present-day Brazil was discovered by the Portuguese in 1500 and developed during the sixteenth and seventeenth centuries as Europe's main source of sugar. From the 1690s important gold deposits began to be discovered and worked in the interior. Because Brazil's Indians were less numerous than Spanish America's, the Portuguese relied more heavily on the labour of African slaves. By the 1820s about 23 per cent of Brazil's population of four million was white, 18 per cent mixed race, 50 per cent black, and 9 per cent Indian (Skidmore and Smith 1997: 25).

The racial composition of Latin American colonial society differed markedly from the patterns found in other European overseas territories. In the thirteen British North American colonies that eventually became the United States, whites were an overwhelming majority and the Indians a marginal element by the eighteenth century. Black slaves accounted for about 10 per cent of the population. Alternatively, in colonial Asia and Africa whites usually remained a very small minority, unable to retain power when indigenous anti-European nationalism gathered strength after 1900. In Latin America whites and *mestizos* led the movements against Spanish and Portuguese colonial rule that brought to independence all of the region, except Spain's Caribbean islands, between 1808 and the mid-1820s.[2] Latin American societies have remained more or less racially diverse and stratified to this day.

Despite their apparent natural advantages – rich mineral deposits and extensive areas of fertile land – the Latin American colonies did not achieve sustained growth in output per head of population, or in manufacturing and commercial activity as a share of output. By the early nineteenth century the region's economic development compared unfavourably with that of Britain or the United States, where rapid industrialization was in progress.

Spanish America's extensive territories had proved difficult to administer effectively, and vulnerable to attack from predatory European rivals: the Dutch, the French, and the British. In both Spanish America and Brazil heavy taxation limited savings and investment. Legal restrictions and poor transport facilities limited trade. The Inquisition conducted by the Catholic church against heresy discouraged scientific thought. Most large estates were farmed carelessly. Salaried managers, deputizing for absentee owners, supervised poorly motivated coerced labourers, usually conscripted or indebted Indians in the Spanish colonies and black slaves in Brazil. Poverty prevented the Indian communities which still controlled about half of Spanish America's agricultural land from improving their methods (Williamson 1992: 119–32, 183–90).

Latin American economic retardation was perpetuated for several decades after independence by chronic political instability. The creole elites which had shaken off European rule were split between 'conservatives' who wanted to maintain established institutions, and 'liberals' who sought modernizing reform, for example by cutting back the privileges of the Catholic church. Frontier disputes broke out between several of the successor states. Mexico lost a third of its national territory (present-day California, Arizona, New Mexico, and Texas) to the expansionist USA. The wars of independence had severely damaged the silver mines, a main source of tax revenue during the colonial period, so governments now lacked sufficient income. Effective authority often passed to individual strongmen (*caudillos*) whose power derived from the ownership of large landed estates and from personal command over fighting men (Halperin Donghi 1993: 42–114; Bulmer-Thomas 1994: 19–45).

Disorder persisted until the second half of the nineteenth century. Hitherto the region's exports had been limited to silver, gold, and the few other items, such as sugar from coastal Brazil and the Caribbean, which could bear the cost of shipment to distant markets. Then from about 1850 the demand generated by Western European and US industrialization, combined with the cheaper transport offered by railways and steam shipping, made it feasible for Latin America to send out a greater range and volume of bulk cargoes, including coffee, wool, grain, meat, cotton, nitrates, and base metals. However, landowners could only profit from these new opportunities by accepting strong central government, to secure property, mobilize labour, and attract outside money for building railways and other essential infrastructure. Some *caudillos* tried to hold out against this new model of political economy, but once in motion the system usually had an irresistible momentum. The growth of foreign trade enlarged governments' tax revenues, and loans from European and US financiers, reassured by the better business prospects. Adequately paid and equipped national armies, now often with railways at their disposal, could crush regional opposition, further improving investment conditions, state finances, and domestic security.

By 1900 most Latin American countries were controlled by restricted groups of large landowners, dedicated to export expansion through collaboration with foreign capitalists, and subscribing, formally at least, to the principles of laissez-faire economic liberalism, imported from Europe. According to this doctrine international free trade maximized prosperity, by allowing each country to specialize in products for which its resources were best suited, following the principles of comparative advantage. So Latin America should export raw materials in return for European and US manufactured goods. State intervention in the national economy should be kept to a minimum. The main function of government was to uphold law and order, allowing private enterprise to flourish. In practice, however, the dominant elites often secured government help when it was likely to be profitable for them, including highly illiberal repressive measures against social inferiors. Characteristic ruling oligarchies included the coffee planters of Brazil's São Paulo region, the leading influence in the country's First Republic (1889–1930), and Argentina's *estancieros*, their fortunes based on the production of wool, grain, and beef. Some governments were dominated more completely by a single man. In Mexico, where the post-independence political instability had been particularly severe, Porfirio Díaz held office as president almost continuously from 1876 until 19ll.

The export booms enriched Latin America's elites, but brought little benefit to the population at large. Over the nineteenth century as a whole average, output per head did not rise significantly; in terms of economic development the region fell further behind Western Europe and North America. Liberal ideology was used as a pretext for taking collectively held land from Indian communities and adding it to the *haciendas*. The strengthened armies and police forces were put at the service of employers in recruiting and disciplining workers. Cash crops for sale overseas encroached on the growing of food for local consumption. Competition from cheaper factory-made goods, imported or national, destroyed handicrafts and the employment which they provided. The widening income disparities between rich and poor held back industrialization by limiting the demand for simple manufactures. The elites preferred luxury imports (Bulmer-Thomas 1994: 83–154, 410–14).

Nevertheless, some industrial and commercial growth did occur in Latin America, fostering urban 'middle sectors' that eventually became strong enough to challenge the export oligarchies. With growing affluence the elites required more doctors, lawyers, shopkeepers, and other functionaries. Estate owners were reluctant to tax their own income or property, so they unintentionally fostered industrialization by using duties on imported goods as a main source of government revenue.

Exports often required some processing before being shipped abroad. Transport equipment had to be maintained. For example, the establishment of meat-packing plants (*frigoríficos*) and railway repair workshops contributed to the growth of Buenos Aires, Argentina's capital.

As urban populations became more numerous, they grew increasingly self confident, assertive, and critical of elite rule, with its alleged subordination of national interests to foreigners. The Mexican Revolution (1910–20) provided a reforming, nationalist example for Latin America as a whole. World War I limited the supply of imported manufactured goods and gave some extra encouragement to industrialization within the region. The next major impetus to social and political change was provided by the international economic depression that followed the 1929 New York stock exchange crash. Although Latin America's foreign trade fell sharply, in most of the region's larger countries economic activity soon recovered. The decline of raw material exports made imported manufactures scarcer and more expensive, so national industry grew faster than before, by enlarging its share of the home market. Then World War II revived export earnings. Latin America lay at a distance from the main theatres of armed conflict, comparatively well placed to help meet the demands of the US and its allies for metals, oil, and other strategic materials (Bulmer-Thomas 1994: 155–257).

Latin American manufacturing growth accelerated after 1945, with increasingly active government support through deliberate policies of import substituting industrialization (ISI). Higher protective duties and new controls were imposed to exclude foreign manufactures. Public enterprises were made responsible for some of the more ambitious industrial projects. At first state-supported ISI yielded impressive results, but by the later 1950s the strategy had begun to show various limitations. The new or enlarged industries were quite successful in meeting national demand for the simpler consumer products, but required considerable imports of machinery and raw materials. As world commodity prices began to fall after the end of the Korean War in 1953, Latin American earnings from raw material exports failed to keep pace with import needs, and many countries incurred persistent balance of payments deficits. Higher inflation impaired the competitiveness of Latin American exports, aggravating balance of payments problems. Social conflict intensified as workers struggled to secure pay increases that would offset anticipated declines in the value of money. By the early 1960s ISI was in crisis.

Latin American countries responded with a range of adjustments or reforms, their detail and emphasis differing according to local circumstances (Chapters 2, 4). Nevertheless, although economic growth continued during the 1960s and 1970s, balance of payments deficits widened further, so by 1980 Latin America had become heavily reliant on loans from foreign banks. Then the region suffered a severe recession, precipitated by a downturn in the world economy, depressed prices for raw material exports, and higher international interest rates. The debt crisis caused widespread disillusionment with ISI as a development strategy, in its various modified forms pursued since the 1960s. Also foreign creditors were able to impose their view that efficiency would be improved by reducing government intervention and opening up national economies to competitive forces. Thus a fashion for economic liberalization took hold in Latin America during the later 1980s, cutting back the protective tariffs, the state agencies, and the state controls built up since 1945. Yet so far the results from liberalization have been disappointing. In most Latin American countries output per head fell during the 1980s, the region's 'lost decade'. The early 1990s brought a modest recovery, but this was threatened in 1994–5 by renewed financial difficulties, and the outlook is uncertain (Bulmer-Thomas 1994: 155–409).

Latin American attempts to promote economic development since 1945 have been accompanied by persistent political instability. Although there are considerable differences between countries, the common sequence runs as follows. As a result of the post-1929 crisis in world trade and finance, many ruling export oligarchies lost power, often through a military coup. With the growth of manufacturing and of cities, governments increasingly took on a populist character. They represented, or claimed to represent, a broad coalition of mainly urban supporters: the professional and service middle classes, industrialists, and manual workers. Populist leaders based their appeal on nationalist measures against foreign business interests, and rhetorical attacks against landowning elites, condemned as 'backward', 'feudal', and the foreigners' allies. However, few substantive measures were taken to break up the big landed estates, and conservative landowners remained a significant political force, especially when they could enlist support from the middle classes and the military, alarmed at populist excesses. Mexico (1910–20) and Bolivia (1952) were exceptional in undergoing broadly based revolutionary upheavals that yielded major agrarian reforms, though even here considerable inequalities in landownership remained. Then in 1959 forces led by Fidel Castro overthrew the Cuban dictator Batista. Castro's regime soon became socialist, closely allying Cuba with the Soviet Union against the

United States, and broadcasting revolutionary propaganda to the rest of Latin America.

The threat from Cuba and the crisis of ISI provoked military coups against elected civilian governments in Brazil (1964) and Argentina (1962, 1966). The 'bureaucratic-authoritarian' military regimes established here claimed to be above politics, and capable of putting ISI on a more disciplined, sustainable basis, by imposing austerity programmes. Elsewhere, for example in Peru (1968) and Ecuador (1972), the military took charge, committed to a more 'left-populist' line. In Chile disappointment with civilian politicians' attempts at moderate reform during the 1960s led in 1970 to the election as president of Salvador Allende, a professed Marxist. After three turbulent years, power was seized by an especially harsh military dictatorship, led by General Pinochet. Mexico gave an impression of stability under its governing party (the *PRI*), established by the 1910–20 revolution. However, economic difficulties and social discontent weakened the *PRI*'s authority, so policy implementation became increasingly erratic.

In most of the small Central American republics restricted landholding elites were still dominant, often ruling through the armed forces. A single family, the Somozas, controlled Nicaragua. During the 1960s and 1970s these oligarchies had to contend with growing popular unrest, mainly in the form of rural and peasant-based uprisings. The Sandinista guerrillas overthrew Nicaragua's Somoza regime in 1979. Rural insurrectionary movements also affected parts of Colombia, Peru, and Mexico. In the Southern Cone (Argentina, Uruguay, Chile) ultra-left 'urban guerrillas' were more conspicuous. The kidnappings, bombings, and armed attacks perpetrated by these small groups of young, predominantly middle class, activists served as another pretext for military intervention, to root out terrorism (Skidmore and Smith 1997; Halperin Donghi 1993: 292–400).

Since the early 1980s violent social conflict has moderated over most of the region, and politics have become less sharply polarized. The debt crisis brought a return to democracy as discredited military regimes gave up office. Their civilian successors have been cautious and restrained, by the standards of pre-1960 populism. Presidents have secured re-election, despite implementing painful measures for economic stabilization. Urban guerrilla activity, effectively crushed by 1980, shows no signs of revival. There are doubts concerning Mexico, where single-party rule has not yet given way to democratic pluralism, but for Latin America as a whole it seems that political instability may have abated, at least for the time being. Perhaps painful experience has established a more secure consensus, bringing to an end the abrupt swings between populist, authoritarian, and radical alternatives that characterized the 1945–80 period.

Table 1.1 gives some recent indicators of Latin America's economic standing. Output per head of population is estimated on a purchasing power parity basis, which takes account of international differences in price levels. (For comparative purposes this method is preferable to calculations of the type often used, based on national currencies at official or market exchange rates.)

The averages for Latin America cover quite wide variations between the richer and poorer countries, for example between Venezuela (1990 output per head $6,740) or Mexico ($5,980) and Honduras ($1,610) or Bolivia ($1,910). Latin America's output per head is much lower than that of the developed 'First World'. Yet despite the problems of the 1980s, at the end of the decade the region was still quite prosperous by the standards of 'Third World' developing countries. Latin America's output per head grew roughly three-fold between 1913 and 1980 (Bulmer-Thomas 1994: 444), an increase similar to the First World's over the same period.

However, other criteria put Latin America in a more unfavourable light. While the region's average output per head in 1990 was still the highest in the Third World, since the 1960s East Asia's has been growing at a much faster rate (Table 1.2). Also the average for East Asia is dominated by China, a large and still relatively poor country

Table 1.1 Comparative indicators of development and welfare, circa 1990

	Output per head (in US $)	Infant mortality rate[a]	Daily calorie supply (per head)
Developing countries	2,296	63	2,523
Latin America	4,769	48	2,721
East Asia	2,390	34	2,617
South Asia[b]	1,218	93	2,215
Sub-Saharan Africa	1,357	107	2,122
Middle East[c]	4,014	79	3,011
Developed countries[d]	17,207	8	3,417
United Kingdom	14,960	8	3,149
United States	21,360	9	3,671

Note: a Number of children dying aged under one year, per 1,000 live births
Note: b India, Pakistan, Bangladesh, Nepal, Sri Lanka, Burma
Note: c Including North Africa
Note: d North America, Western Europe, Japan, Australia, New Zealand
Source World Bank 1992: 272–3, 276–7

(1990 output per head $1,950). Much higher levels of prosperity have been achieved by certain smaller East Asian territories, sometimes referred to as the 'Gang of Four' or 'Baby Tigers': South Korea ($7,190), Taiwan ($9,200), Singapore ($14,920), and Hong Kong ($16,230). The success of these 'newly industrialized countries' (NICs) was associated with the production of manufactured goods for export, and entailed annual growth in output per head at rates of 6–10 per cent. Since the 1970s their pattern of rapid export-led development has been imitated by other East Asian countries, including China. During the 1980s the Gang of Four's economic growth continued almost unchecked. Moreover, Latin America has made less progress than East Asia in raising standards of welfare, such as nutrition and child mortality. Although in 1990 the region's output per head remained considerably above the East Asian average, Latin America's calorie supply per head was only a little higher, and newly born infants there had lower chances of survival (Table 1.1).

Therefore Latin American history is commonly seen as one of 'unfulfilled promise' (Bulmer-Thomas 1994: 410). The region has failed to achieve First World living standards, despite an abundance of natural resources, and has failed to establish a tradition of stable democratic government, despite the ideals proclaimed by the early nineteenth-century independence movements.

Table 1.2 Annual rates of growth in output per head of population: main world regions, 1950–94 (%)

	1950–9	*1960–9*	*1970–9*	*1980–9*	*1990–4*
Developing countries	2.4	3.9	3.1	1.1*	0.2*
Latin America	1.9	2.5	3.0	-0.3	1.8
East Asia	2.7	3.6	5.0	6.3	8.0
South Asia	2.0	1.4	1.2	3.5	2.0
Sub-Saharan Africa	1.2	0.6	1.1	-1.3	-1.8
Middle East	1.8	6.0	3.1	-2.9	-0.5
Developed countries	3.0	4.1	2.4	-2.6	1.0

Note: *These figures include the former Soviet Union and the former Soviet bloc countries of Eastern Europe

Sources World Bank 1984b: 486; World Bank 1992: 32; World Bank 1995: 164–5, 210–11; World Bank 1996: 195, 209

THEORETICAL PERSPECTIVES

The chapter so far has concentrated on matters of fact. We shall now raise issues of interpretation, by sketching out various theories or explanations that may be relevant to understanding Latin America's current difficulties and its historical past.

During the oligarchical period Latin American elites hoped to improve their countries' relative economic status by promoting exports. However, it was widely believed that severe, perhaps insuperable obstacles to achieving US or Western European levels of development were posed by the effects of the tropical climate in discouraging hard work, and by the natural inferiority of the region's large non-white populations. Such climatic or racial determinism is no longer accepted.

Structuralism

A more sophisticated approach was offered by structuralism, a body of thinking developed in the 1940s and 1950s to justify ISI. The theory came to be particularly associated with the Argentine economist Raul Prebisch and one of the main vehicles for his influence, the Economic Commission for Latin America (ECLA), a United Nations agency established in 1948. (The term structuralism derived from a subsidiary argument, which attributed the high inflation often generated by ISI to aspects of Latin American economic *structure*.) Prebisch argued that for various reasons Latin America was suffering from a long-term decline in the price of its raw material exports relative to the price of the manufactured goods imported from the advanced industrial economies. The share of food and other basic commodities in developed countries' consumer spending was declining as incomes rose. Synthetic substitutes were being developed for many raw materials. The limited number of industrial firms made possible monopolistic or semi-monopolistic restraints on price competition, and industrial workers were organized in powerful trade unions. Therefore while in manufacturing technical progress benefited producers, through higher profits and wages, in primary commodity sectors technical progress benefited consumers, through lower prices. This invalidated the claim of liberal economists that all countries gained equally from free world trade and the international division of labour, according to the principle of comparative advantage. Latin America had been affected by a pattern of 'unequal exchange'. The region could only escape from its subordinate, 'peripheral' status and catch up with the developed 'centre' by strengthening its own industry, using whatever degree of government support might be required (Bethell 1994a: 393–432).

Modernization theory

Structuralist analysis and ISI policy received support during the 1950s from the 'modernization theory' expounded by many US-based social scientists, who assumed that Latin American countries (and the Third World as a whole) were beginning a process of change already completed by the advanced industrial countries. The introduction of superior First World technologies would raise production per head. Industry's share of national output would rise, and agriculture's would decline. The growth of towns would allow people to escape from the ignorance and apathy allegedly characteristic of 'traditional' rural life, dominated in Latin America by archaic 'feudal' estates, to become more educated, ambitious, innovative, and enterprising. 'Modernized' social attitudes, rising prosperity, and a growing middle class, would provide a secure basis for democracy, as an alternative to 'traditional' dictatorships and oligarchies (Cubitt 1995: 32–5).

However, in the 1960s both structuralism and modernization theory came to be seen as over-optimistic. Apart from ISI's obvious economic weaknesses, its social and political consequences also caused alarm. The opportunities offered by industrialization attracted waves of migrants into the towns from the countryside, though the new factories provided employment for only a small minority. Millions had to eke out a living from casual 'informal-sector' occupations, for example street trading or building work, and find housing in the shanty towns that proliferated around the major cities. Urbanization of this type did not offer a likely basis for the smooth, conflict-free progress envisaged by modernization theory. The advent of bureaucratic-authoritarian military regimes contradicted arguments that economic development would strengthen democracy.

Dependency theory

These trends stimulated the formulation of dependency theory, quasi-Marxist and strongly anti-capitalist in its assumptions. Dependency theory also drew encouragement from a general radical mood, inspired by the Cuban Revolution, by the campaign for black civil rights in the US, and by opposition to US military involvement in Vietnam. *Dependentistas* accepted the ECLA thesis that ISI was necessary to end the 'unequal exchange' which Latin America had suffered in its foreign trade. However, they rejected structuralist attempts to base development on partnership between government and a private capitalist sector. In practice, Latin American industrialization had come to rely heavily on manufacturing investment by large US and European firms, the so-called multinational or transnational corporations (MNCs, TNCs). According to dependency theory the MNCs used monopoly power to extract large profits and royalty payments from the countries in which they operated. The firms equipped their Latin American branch factories with costly imported machinery, devised for use in developed economies where high wage levels required labour-saving technology. Thus further pressure was put on Latin America's balance of payments. The investment created few jobs, but superseded existing labour-intensive operations, so instead of the widely spread prosperity anticipated by modernization theory, unemployment and inequality were made worse. MNC penetration displaced or incorporated nationally owned firms, preventing profit accumulation for reinvestment in Latin America and the growth there of a middle class. The swing towards authoritarian military rule in the 1960s was interpreted as resulting from the concern of narrow indigenous 'collaborating elites' to reassure their foreign allies by repressing national labour movements. Dependency theory was first evolved for Latin America, and then applied to Third World countries in general. It claimed that they could only achieve true development through socialist revolution and exit from the international capitalist economy, following the Cuban and Chinese examples (Bethell 1994a: 432–54; Cubitt 1995: 35–41).

After enjoying a phase of influence during the later 1960s and early 1970s, dependency theory fell into disrepute. The enthusiasm for radical causes characteristic of the period waned. Attempts at putting ideas of socialist self-sufficiency into practice had disappointing results on Cuba, for example, and disastrous effects elsewhere, most notoriously in Cambodia and Ethiopia. Above all, the increasingly conspicuous success of the East Asian NICs, based on vigorous participation in the international economy, challenged the assumption that First World capitalism is a malign, exploitative force, from which the Third World should distance itself.

Neoliberalism

The decline of dependency theory has been balanced by the resurgence of free-market ideology, now usually termed neoliberalism. In the developed countries liberal laissez-faire was discredited by the depression of the 1930s and by the effectiveness of government action in mobilizing resources during World War II. Thus after 1945 opinion favoured a 'mixed' economy, combining capitalism with substantial state participation and management. The consensus lasted until about 1970, when the US and Western Europe began to experience declining rates of output growth, accompanied by rising inflation and unemployment. The malaise could be plausibly attributed to excessive government 'interference', so economic liberalism came back into favour, after surviving for the duration as a minority faith in academic circles. The neoliberal programme, known from its political leaders as 'Thatcherism' in Britain, and 'Reaganomics' in the United States, aimed at reinvigorating capitalist enterprise, by tax cuts, deregulation, and the transfer of state undertakings to private ownership (privatization).

These successive currents of First World opinion reached Latin America, and the Third World at large. The fashion for state intervention established in the 1940s encouraged ECLA structuralist ideas and ISI policies; its erosion three decades later encouraged the turn towards economic liberalization. Neoliberalism has gained ground in Latin America partly through local disillusionment with ISI, brought to a head by the debt crisis. Also, many Latin American economists are trained at US or Western European universities. Finally, since 1982 Latin America's financial plight has given leverage to the US government, working together with the IMF (International Monetary Fund) and the World Bank, agencies headquartered in Washington, D. C.. This coalition urging neoliberal reforms on developing countries, as a prerequisite for further loans, is sometimes termed the Washington consensus (Williamson 1990).

Neoliberals admire the East Asian model of rapid outward-looking development, and recommend it as an example for Latin America to follow. They cite the policy reforms initiated about 1960 by Taiwan and South Korea which repudiated ISI and launched manufacturing export drives. According to the neoliberal analysis, at least in its more dogmatic versions, these countries' subsequent economic success was achieved by minimizing detailed government intervention, with the 'distortions' which it causes, and allowing market forces free play (Balassa *et al.* 1986). Thus, it is alleged, the basis was laid for vigorous export-led growth. In contrast, Latin America suffered because policy there remained too inward-looking and interventionist.

East Asia's economic dynamism has helped to discredit dependency theory, but there are many who dislike the neoliberal alternative, and challenge its gloss on the region's recent history. Critics of neoliberalism will be referred to here as statists. They have collected evidence that governments took a highly active role in East Asian industrialization, a point that some neoliberals concede, especially for South Korea

(World Bank 1987: 71). Therefore the real contrast may not be between East Asia's free market success and futile Latin American *dirigisme*, but between effective East Asian and ineffective Latin American state intervention. If so, then further problems arise. What specific measures have proved most useful? And why should governments have been better able to sustain them in East Asia than in Latin America? Debate over these matters, conducted through comparison of the two regions, has informed much work on recent Latin American history (Banuri 1991; Gereffi and Wyman 1990; Haggard 1990; Hewitt *et al.* 1992; Lin 1989; Morawetz 1981), and the comparative theme recurs at a number of points in this book. Of the four original 'Baby Tigers', the city states Hong Kong and Singapore are quite distinctive in structure, so South Korea and more occasionally Taiwan will serve as the main East Asian reference points. The East Asian NICs and most Latin American countries shared the same general objectives, of achieving economic development and rising income per head through industrialization. However, East Asia's strategies differed from Latin America's in their detail, and proved much more successful.

Post-modernism

Neoliberalism focuses on economics, and discussion of the issues that it raises has involved economists and economic historians. Other disciplines (political science, sociology, social anthropology) that were for a time receptive to the dependency approach, have coped with its decline by drawing on innovations in philosophy, linguistics, and literary analysis, commonly termed post-modernism, to argue that no all-embracing theory can accommodate the cultural diversity of human behaviour. This view contrasts with Marxist interpretations, which categorized society in terms of a few classes, based on economic interest, and made conflict between them determine historical change. Though generally radical/left in spirit, and strongly hostile to neoliberalism, the post-modernist perspective is loosely defined and eclectic. It takes a sympathetic interest in a wide variety of subordinate popular elements, often localized and small-scale, which challenge 'establishment' capitalist orthodoxy. They include neighbourhood self-help groups among the poor, and activists on environmental issues. There is also a related concern with gender and with women's role in society, preoccupations of the feminist movement that derived from the 1960s' radical upsurge. Writers influenced by post-modernist thinking believe that the recent proliferation in Latin America of local-level movements, often involving women, indigenous peoples, and other hitherto marginalized categories, represents a hopeful trend. Perhaps grass-roots, 'bottom up' approaches to development needs can succeed where clumsy, technocratic, 'top down' projects failed (Cubitt 1995: 47–9; Green 1991; Green 1995: 192–6).

PLAN OF THIS BOOK

The following discussion has these issues in mind. The primary subject is recent economic history, but we must locate the economics within a larger set of interrelated themes, and recognize how modern phenomena often have more remote historical origins. Chapter 2 pursues the topic of economic development, defined narrowly as the growth in output per head of population. (The welfare aspects of development are considered separately, in Chapter 5.) ISI as pursued in Latin America after 1945 proved a deeply flawed strategy, inferior to the more outward looking, export-oriented approach adopted by the East Asian NICs. As a result Latin America became over-reliant on foreign capital, and was severely affected by the debt crisis of the early 1980s. However, the neoliberal remedies applied in the region have had major limitations as a basis for securing recovery, and partly for this reason the post-1980 economic slow-down has been prolonged.

Chapter 3 examines the position of Latin America in the wider world. While dependency theory as an elaborated general doctrine is no longer persuasive, many still consider that the region has suffered particular disadvantages in its international relations, perhaps through the close proximity of the US as a regional superpower. One survey concludes that, in the aftermath of the debt crisis, Latin America will 'have to continue to cope with the implications of subordination and dependency' (Skidmore and Smith 1997: 424). Another widely used text claims that Latin America's recent economic and social crises 'have given new relevance to the dependency approach' (Keen 1996: xi). However, it is argued here that external pressures should not be seen as a primary cause of the region's difficulties since 1945.

Chapter 4 therefore reviews the course of social change and political conflict within Latin America over the last half century. Political instability has resulted above all from the failure of governments to satisfy aspirations for sustained economic growth, in a region marked by exceptionally wide disparities between rich and poor. Such inequality derived originally from the racial stratification and concentrated landownership established by a distinctive pattern of European rule, but has been aggravated by ISI. Unstable, erratic government has in turn further impaired economic performance. Latin America differs markedly on this point from East Asia, where for historical reasons societies are more cohesive, homogeneous, and egalitarian, and where strong, purposeful governments have been better able to implement coherent development strategies (Gereffi and Wyman 1990: 139–204).

Latin American inequality has had other economic consequences, through its effects on social welfare (Chapter 5). With a large share of income going to wealthy elites, much of the population has been left without adequate health care and education, to the detriment of labour efficiency. A criticism levelled against liberalization is that it aggravates the problem of labour force 'quality', by requiring cuts in government spending and other adjustments that fall most severely on the poor. Neoliberals reply that their policies will promote welfare through the employment generated by labour-intensive economic growth of the East Asian type. They also argue that the poor can be protected from spending reductions by deploying available resources more selectively. In fact, some social indicators have continued to improve since the early 1980s, even when average income per head has fallen. Local-level popular action may have limited the damaging welfare effects of the debt crisis, partly justifying the post-modernist left's stress of the value of grassroots mobilization. However, 'bottom up' initiatives cannot by themselves go very far towards solving the region's development problems.

The period since 1945 has brought some improvement in the status of Latin American women (Chapter 6). However, the social progress represented by female emancipation may also entail economic costs. Considerable use has been made of women workers in East Asian manufacturing, where they have been obliged by patriarchal, discriminatory attitudes to accept rigorous discipline, and much lower rates of pay than those received by equally skilled men. In Latin American industry, on the other hand, female participation has remained relatively low, a significant competitive disadvantage. Furthermore, over the last twenty years feminist movements have grown up in the region, their position enhanced by the return to democratic politics. This is probably limiting the recruitment of Latin American women as cheap, flexible, docile labour for export manufacturing, along East Asian lines.

Recently Latin American environmental issues (Chapter 7) have attracted much notice, especially through First World concern over the destruction of the Amazonian rainforest. The road building, cattle ranching, power generation, and mining projects associated with deforestation may represent examples of the misdirected investment that led to the debt crisis of the early 1980s. Accelerating environmental degradation may have played an important role in aggravating the subsequent recession, although this point is open to dispute.

The book concludes with some remarks on Latin America's current situation, in the light of the historical record (Chapter 8). Neoliberals claim that the economic upturn achieved by the region since 1991 shows that their recommendations are finally bearing fruit. Critics of neoliberalism are still highly sceptical. It is suggested here that while there are grounds for guarded optimism, deep-seated structural problems remain which will prevent Latin America from matching East Asia's economic dynamism.

Latin America is a large and diverse region. This short study cannot do justice to the great range of variation between particular countries, and therefore concentrates on establishing general themes, sometimes illustrated with national cases. Brazil under its 1964–85 military regime provides the most conspicuous example of a 'development dictatorship' pursuing ISI, and for a time apparently enjoying some success with the strategy. Argentina has been noted for its economic retardation, chronic social conflict, and powerful trade union movement. In Chile special domestic circumstances led to unusually vigorous neoliberal measures, perhaps with some useful results. Cuba illustrates the hopes and disappointments of a socialist revolution. There are several excellent books which detail the contrasting histories of individual Latin American countries at greater length (Bethell 1991; Keen 1996; Sheahan 1987; Skidmore and Smith 1997; Williamson 1992; Wynia 1990).

NOTES

1 The term 'Indian' is employed here for the region's indigenous people, following normal Latin American usage. However, in English-speaking countries the alternatives 'native American', 'indigenous American', or 'Amerindian' are now often preferred.

2 Some definitions of Latin America include Haiti, formerly the French colony of Saint-Domingue. However, this book considers only those territories that were under Spanish or Portuguese rule until the early nineteenth century, excluding Puerto Rico, taken by the US from Spain in 1898. The Dominican Republic finally gained its independence from Spain in 1865; Cuba did so in 1898.

2 Economic development

Latin America as a whole achieved rapid economic growth from the 1950s until the early 1980s, followed by a severe recession and a weak recovery. However, within this general pattern the experience of particular countries varied (Table 2.1). For example, between 1950 and 1980 Brazil had the region's highest growth rate, while Argentina had the lowest. Colombia was less affected than its neighbours by the 1980s debt crisis. Chile suffered badly, but improved its performance towards the end of the decade. In the 1990s that country became Latin America's one notable economic success. East Asia's growth has been more rapid and better sustained than Latin America's.

Major changes have occurred in economic structure (Table 2.2). The relative importance of industry in Latin America grew rapidly from

Table 2.1 Annual rates of growth in output per head of population: Latin America and East Asia, 1950–94 (%)

	1950–9	1960–9	1970–9	1980–9	1990–6
Latin America	1.9	2.5	3.0	-0.3	1.3
Argentina	0.9	2.7	0.6	-1.8	2.9
Brazil	3.6	3.2	6.2	0.7	0.6
Chile	1.8	2.0	0.7	2.4	4.2
Colombia	1.5	2.1	3.6	1.8	2.6
Mexico	2.5	4.2	2.1	-1.0	nil
Peru	2.9	1.8	0.4	-2.4	0.6
East Asia	2.7	3.6	5.0	6.3	8.0
South Korea	3.0	5.8	7.8	8.2	6.0

Sources World Bank 1984b: 486–8; World Bank 1992: 32; World Bank 1995: 164–5, 210–11; World Bank 1996: 194–5, 208–9; Green 1995: 211–43; *The Economist* 1996, 1997

the 1930s, a trend that slowed after 1955, and was reversed after 1980. Exports' share of regional output declined after 1930, and made a very slight recovery after 1970, with a modest increase in the contribution coming from manufactured goods. In South Korea, representing the East Asian experience, rapid industrialization did not begin until the 1950s. It was associated after 1960 with a very marked shift towards manufacturing for export.

Brazil and Mexico are by a wide margin Latin America's two largest economies, accounting in 1994 for 52 per cent of the region's population and 57 per cent of its output. These countries have reached levels of development slightly above the regional average. Argentina, Uruguay, Chile, and Venezuela, are also relatively prosperous. The poorer countries include Peru, Bolivia, Paraguay, Ecuador, Colombia, and the small Central American republics (see map). Although agriculture's share of Latin American output fell sharply after 1930, the sector retained a considerable proportion of the workforce: about 50 per cent in the 1950s, and 25 per cent in the 1980s. Labour productivity

Table 2.2 Changes in economic structure: Latin America and South Korea, 1955–94

	% Share of GDP				*Manufactures share of exports (%)*
	Agriculture	*Industry*	*Services*	*Exports*	
Latin America					
1930[a]	45	15	40	30	n.a.
1955	20	32	48	12	n.a.
1960	16	31	53	15	5
1970	12	35	53	13	8
1980	10	38	50	16	30
1994	10	33	55	15	34[b]
South Korea					
1955	45	16	39	2	n.a.
1960	37	20	43	3	19
1970	27	30	44	14	77
1980	15	40	45	34	89
1994	7	43	50	36	93

Note: a The figures for this year are rough estimates
Note: b Estimate for 1989
Sources World Bank 1984b: 502–5, 510–13; World Bank 1995: 190–1;
World Bank 1996: 211; Bulmer-Thomas 1994: 9, 192–5, 226

in Latin America's agriculture is much lower than in its industry, an important cause of the wide income inequalities that characterize the region (Chapter 4).

The following discussion considers the trends indicated by Tables 2.1 and 2.2, with particular reference to issues raised in Chapter 1. Why, despite the growing difficulties encountered by ISI during the 1950s, did Latin America not shift to a more export-based economic strategy, as happened in East Asia? Why, after two further decades of essentially inward-oriented development, was Latin America affected by such a severe crisis of foreign indebtedness during the 1980s? Was excessive government interventionism in pursuit of ISI the main cause of Latin America's difficulties? If so, then why have neoliberal reforms not yet brought a robust economic recovery?

INWARD VERSUS OUTWARD ORIENTATION

ISI, the drive for economic self-sufficiency begun by the larger Latin American countries during the 1930s, and by South Korea and Taiwan after World War II, aimed to replace imported goods with nationally produced manufactures. However, many of the newly established industries proved to be high-cost and inefficient, partly as a result of technical inexperience, a weakness that might be remedied with the passage of time, but also because the limited size of national markets prevented factories from working at full capacity or achieving economies of large-scale operation. Rising expenditures on imported capital goods (steel, machinery, etc.) and raw materials, together with the stagnation of traditional commodity exports, put severe pressure on the balance of payments. From about 1960 South Korea and Taiwan sought to solve these problems by giving up comprehensive ISI and concentrating instead on turning out a more limited range of goods for export, mainly to the developed countries. Export sales would enable firms to escape the confines of a small national market, and produce on a more extensive, more efficient scale. At first the emphasis was put on simple, labour-intensive products (textiles, clothing, shoes, toys), to take full advantage of low East Asian wage costs. However, the rapid growth of output and the demand for labour soon caused wage rates to rise. Manufacturers responded by moving into more advanced, capital-intensive lines (consumer electronics, chemicals, engineering). Export earnings provided the means to upgrade, by importing equipment and technology from the developed countries. International competitive pressures stimulated continuing improvements in business methods. Thus outward-looking growth continued as a dynamic, self-reinforcing process, with the benefits spread widely among the population at large, through the employment generated by manufacturing (Balassa *et al.* 1986).

In Latin America, on the other hand, although during the 1960s some countries initiated measures to encourage manufactured exports, for various reasons the shift towards an externally oriented development strategy was less decisive than in South Korea or Taiwan. Export promotion, at least in its early stages, required the strict control of wage levels, to keep the 'cheap-labour' advantage. Latin America's political circumstances and habits of trade union militancy made this difficult (Chapter 4). Also, the need for radical adjustment seemed less urgent than in the East Asian NICs, because other promising options were available. For the main Latin American republics, with their relatively large populations and abundant natural resources, it was apparently feasible to 'deepen' ISI, by building up national capacity in the more sophisticated capital goods industries, and dispensing with foreign suppliers. Latin American governments had neglected agriculture, so it was thought that greater attention to the sector's problems would be rewarding. Agrarian reform schemes were devised, to take underused land from large estates for sharing out as smaller holdings, which it was hoped would be farmed more intensively by the new owners. Land reform was intended to increase agricultural output, thus easing inflationary and balance of payments pressures. Income would be distributed less unequally, thus enlarging the domestic market for ISI undertakings, and allowing them to bring underused capacity into full operation. Increasing the number of property owners counteracted the threat of subversion from Cuba. (South Korea and Taiwan had already completed thorough land reforms by the 1960s, and agricultural improvement did not offer large dividends.) Much was expected in Latin America from regional trade agreements between neighbouring countries, which would allow local firms to increase their sales volumes behind a high common external tariff (Bulmer-Thomas 1994: 297–322).

Nevertheless, these partial modifications to ISI had disappointing results, problems of industrial inefficiency persisted, and the long-term deterioration in Latin America's balance of trade continued. During the 1960s deficits were covered partly through US government aid or loans, increased in response to the Cuban Revolution, and through MNC investment. However, by the end of the decade these sources were becoming insufficient. The MNCs faced growing hostility from nationalist opinion, influenced by dependency theory, while the US was less willing to provide official funds because of its costly war in

Vietnam. At the same time the evolution of new international banking techniques made 'non-official' loans from developed country commercial banks more readily available. The volume of such loans grew rapidly after the Organization of Petroleum Exporting Countries (OPEC) raised the price of oil from US $3 to $12 per barrel in 1973–4, and to $30 in 1979. OPEC members deposited much of their revenues to earn interest in First World banks. The recessions caused in the developed countries by the oil shocks limited investment opportunities there, and bankers turned to the Third World, Latin America in particular, as an outlet for surplus funds. Most Latin American countries depended on imported oil, so the sudden increases in its price widened balance of payments deficits. Mexico, Venezuela, and Ecuador benefited as oil exporters, but borrowed heavily on the strength of future income to finance ambitious government spending programmes. Thus Latin America's external debt grew ten-fold during the 1970s, and exceeded US $300 billion by 1982.

Then Mexico announced that payments on its foreign debt could not be maintained, damaging confidence in other Latin American countries, and drastically curtailing new bank loans. The immediate cause of the debt crisis was the neoliberal 'monetarist' policy adopted by Great Britain and the USA, relying on high interest rates to control inflation. Between 1978 and 1982 the average annual interest rates on foreign bank loans doubled. At the same time world-wide recession cut the demand for Latin American exports, still mainly raw materials. By 1982 service charges on foreign debt absorbed nearly 60 per cent of the region's export earnings, and a sharp reduction of economic activity was necessary to limit the demand for imports (Bethell 1994a: 200–37; Bulmer-Thomas 1994: 358–65; Frieden 1991: 59–66).

The East Asian NICs faced the same international circumstances, but coped with them more easily. Hong Kong and Taiwan had been running large balance of payments surpluses, and so were not indebted. Singapore had drawn in foreign capital through MNC investment rather than bank loans. South Korea had borrowed heavily; relative to national output its debt was greater than Mexico's or Brazil's. But Korea's exports constituted a larger share of output, and they were predominantly manufactures, less severely affected than raw materials by the recession. So the country could increase its foreign exchange earnings to meet the heavier interest payments, without suffering the 'import strangulation' that affected Latin America after 1982 (Bulmer-Thomas 1994: 363–409; Banuri 1991: 66–7).

Neoliberals therefore argue that East Asia's externally oriented industrialization has proved inherently superior to Latin America's modified ISI of the 1960s and 1970s: more efficient, and less vulnerable to external shocks. Some statists question this thesis by claiming that the historical record for the Third World as a whole shows no clear relationship between outward orientation and economic success, and that selecting a few East Asian instances for comparison with Latin America gives a misleading impression. The East Asian NICs are relatively small: South Korea's population in 1965 was twenty-eight million, Taiwan's was eleven million, and Singapore's was less than two million. Industry here could only achieve an adequate operating scale through export. But for at least the larger Latin American republics, such as Brazil (1965 population eighty-three million) or Mexico (forty-three million), ISI should have been feasible if it had been better managed. India and China are cited as successful examples of ISI in big countries (Banuri 1991: 72–4, 91–5, 102–7). Yet India's economic record is mediocre, while China's growth accelerated markedly when the country began opening itself up to the capitalist world in the 1970s. The Brazilian economy is large by Latin American standards; hence its relatively strong performance during the 1950–80 period (Table 2.1). However, Brazil's national output is still only a third of Great Britain's, and a sixteenth of the USA's, almost certainly too small for efficient ISI.

Quite clearly outward-looking development strategies have proved the best way to secure rapid economic growth. But how should they be pursued? Exactly how did the East Asian NICs succeed as exporters of manufactures, and how might Latin American countries follow their example? On these points there is much more room for debate. All neoliberals emphasize the importance of controlling inflation, to establish macroeconomic stability and a secure, predictable business environment. They are less united and convincing on other issues. Some neoliberals believe that detailed government participation in industry, commonly termed 'industrial policy', is almost invariably futile or damaging; others take a more qualified position. And statists have been able to argue plausibly that industrial policy has proved useful in East Asia. There are similar differences of opinion over tariff and financial liberalization. It is the more uncompromising versions of neoliberalism that have often come to determine policy in Latin America, with doubtful consequences for the future.

MACROECONOMIC STABILITY: INFLATION AND EXCHANGE RATES

Latin America has experienced high inflation. The region's average annual rate of price increase was about 20 per cent in the 1960s, 40 per cent in the 1970s, and 200 per cent in the 1980s. Comparable figures for South Korea are: 17 per cent in the 1960s, 20 per cent in the 1970s, and 5 per cent in the 1980s (Sheahan 1987: 102; Banuri 1991: 17). Neoliberals argue that rapid inflation does considerable harm, by discouraging productive investment and by aggravating business uncertainty. The price level in Latin American countries has often risen rapidly, without appropriate adjustments to foreign exchange rates. Currencies have thus become overvalued, making the region's exports uncompetitive in world markets. Increases in the real effective exchange rate (REER: see Glossary) have limited the development of export sales. Therefore a high priority should be given to establishing price stability, the neglect of which, neoliberals allege, has been a main cause of Latin America's economic difficulties.

Statists have tried to dispute this emphasis. They claim that inflation should be seen as a symptom of more fundamental weaknesses, or a price worth paying to achieve rapid development, and cite instances where a country's exports have grown strongly, despite an appreciating REER (Banuri 1991: 86–8). Such arguments are unconvincing. Certainly within Latin America the relationship between inflation and economic performance is not exact: for example, until the 1980s Brazil had the region's highest rate of output growth, and also relatively high inflation. But there can be no doubt that the very severe inflation which became common in Latin America after the debt crisis has made recovery more difficult, and that over the longer term Latin American exporters have been disadvantaged by REER instability (Bulmer-Thomas 1994: 352–3, 380–1; Lin 1989, 176–82; Morawetz 1981: 39–55).

The shortages of the World War II period pushed up Latin American price levels. Then inflation was perpetuated by the extra protection given under ISI to high-cost, monopolistic national industries. The political weakness of populist governments limited their ability to impose new taxes, or contain the demands of public employees and unionized industrial workers for higher pay. State revenues lagged behind the growth of state spending, and budget deficits were financed by enlarging the money supply. As Latin American inflation remained relatively high by world standards, the region's exports became uncompetitive. One possible response was a devaluation of the national currency. However, post-1945 governments were reluctant to devalue, because doing so benefited traditional export interests (large landowners, foreign mining companies), and made manufacturers' imported inputs more expensive. Indeed, populist policy saw overvaluation as a convenient way of taxing exporters to subsidize ISI. Devaluation was usually postponed until balance of payments difficulties made it unavoidable as a crisis measure, which then aggravated inflation by suddenly raising the cost of essential imports (Bulmer-Thomas 1994: 251–5, 283–7).

Inflationary expectations became so firmly established that they could not be broken even by the more authoritarian regimes that came to power after 1960. For example, Brazil's military dictatorship accommodated inflation by frequent small devaluations to maintain export competitiveness. However, during the 1970s Brazil and several of its neighbours tried unsuccessfully to cushion the impact from the OPEC oil price increases by limiting further devaluations. REERs therefore rose and exports were discouraged. Then the devaluations precipitated by the 1982 debt crisis gave the inflationary spiral an extra twist. The return to democracy allowed organized labour more freedom to force up money earnings. The payment of interest charges on government debt widened budget deficits. In several countries the annual rate of price increase accelerated to more that 1,000 per cent (Bulmer-Thomas 1994: 387–98). Perhaps the threat of uncontrolled hyperinflation has changed public attitudes, at least for the time being. Since 1990 inflation has been curbed, partly because concern over the issue has made electorates more willing to support politicians who implement neoliberal stabilization measures. However, Latin America has certainly been handicapped by its last half century of monetary turbulence.

As a contrast, in South Korea and Taiwan, episodes of hyperinflation during the immediate post-1945 period convinced policy makers of the need for financial restraint, and strong authoritarian governments could put their views into effect. The shift away from ISI during the 1960s occurred against a background of relative price stability, quite unlike Latin America in the 1980s. The inflationary effects from the devaluations that launched the East Asian NICs' export drives were easily contained. Thereafter the basic resilience of the growth process assured financial equilibrium (Lin 1989: 128–90).

INDUSTRIAL POLICY

Statists argue that in developing countries trying to catch up with the First World, governments must actively support manufacturing. Elements of industrial policy include tariff protection, state-owned enterprises (SOEs), and state subsidies for private firms. The more novel and sophisticated industries which are likely to grow rapidly in the future should be given a high priority. They nurture advanced skills and stimulate innovation in related sectors. A strong indigenous technical capability gives extra bargaining power in negotiation with First World suppliers of expertise. The foreign exchange cost of royalty payments on licensed technology is minimized. The East Asian NICs relied on industrial policy as well as market forces to upgrade from the original low-skill, cheap-labour, 'sweat shop' manufacturing export lines. In East Asia governments account for as large a share of national output (about 25 per cent) as in Latin America (Hewitt *et al.* 1992: 97–127).

On the other hand, dogmatic neoliberals assert that active industrial policy, under which governments try to 'pick winners', is almost invariably harmful. State bureaucrats with public funds at their disposal are more likely to be careless in routine management, and to launch over-ambitious, ill-judged schemes than are entrepreneurs who risk their own capital, or executives held to account by shareholders (Balassa *et al.* 1986). For example, after the 1973–4 OPEC oil price shock Brazil embarked on a heavily subsidized project to manufacture ethanol (industrial alcohol) from sugar cane, replacing imported petroleum as fuel for motor vehicles. The ethanol programme turned out to be grossly uneconomic. Borrowing by slackly run SOEs accounts for much of Latin America's foreign debt. Public sector industry may be quite important in East Asia, but the region's SOEs are, compared with Latin America's, more concentrated on infrastructure and utilities (railways, water supply, etc.), than on manufacturing, where profit-conscious leadership is needed to achieve international standards of efficiency (Hewitt *et al.* 1992: 170, 304; Williamson 1990: 16).

However, the East Asian experience suggests that state participation in manufacturing can be useful, as moderate neoliberals acknowledge, if it reinforces a vigorous, competitive private sector and is export-related. For example, the South Korean steel company POSCO was founded in 1970 with government participation, and quickly achieved an efficient operating scale by supplying the country's export-oriented shipbuilding industry. By the 1980s POSCO had become one of the world's lowest-cost steel producers (World Bank 1987: 71). South Korea's shipyards belong to large, conglomerate business corporations (*chaebols*), privately owned, but established with state support after 1945, and responsive to state guidance (Hewitt *et al.* 1992: 115–16). The *chaebols* must compete with each other for market share, executive talent, and official patronage. The Korean state has supervised the *chaebols*' recent moves into the production for export of motor cars and computer memory chips. Government technical leadership has also been important for private-sector industry in Taiwan, where small firms are more typical (Gereffi and Wyman 1990: 231–66).

In contrast, Latin American industrial policy usually aimed at deepening ISI, and so lacked focus. SOEs proliferated, many of them with national monopolies (Bulmer-Thomas 1994: 350–8). Scientific and technical manpower, relatively limited in any case by poor educational provision (Chapter 5), has been spread over too wide a range of objectives. Elite interest groups secured wasteful, corrupt allocations of state funds (Chapter 4), for example, through the cheap credit given to estate owners under Brazil's ethanol programme. Latin American military dictatorships favoured industries with a strategic potential: armaments, aircraft, nuclear power. Projects in such fields were likely to be technically overambitious. Often they developed as jealously guarded fiefs, linked to particular branches of the armed forces, poorly coordinated, and detached from civilian industry (Rouquié 1987: 294–302).

The Washington consensus, neoliberals who acknowledge that industrial policy may have been useful in East Asia, attribute its success there to exceptionally high levels of government competence. Developing countries elsewhere are strongly advised against trying to imitate this aspect of East Asian practice (World Bank 1987: 66–71; Williamson 1990: 28). Latin American adjustment programmes have tackled SOE underperformance by closing down the least viable operations and selling off others. Some remarkable efficiency gains have occurred. However, privatization has served above all as a source of urgently needed revenue for meeting debt payments, and many SOEs have been sold as unregulated monopolies, to maximize the price obtained (Green 1995: 72–6).

THE EXTERNAL TARIFF

Neoliberal policy in Latin America has brought about the rapid dismantling of tariff barriers. Between 1973 and 1979 Chile eliminated import quotas, and cut the average duty from about 100 per cent to 10 per cent. Since the debt crisis most other countries have followed suit. Neoliberal theory predicts that greater competition and freer access to imported inputs should stimulate major improvements in manufacturing efficiency. Firms will be encouraged to specialize and build up foreign sales in lines for which they are best suited. The balance of payments will be strengthened, as exports soon outstrip any initial surge of imports, and long-term output growth will improve.

However, there is so far no clear evidence that Latin America has embarked on export-led 'manufacturing miracles' of the East Asian type. Since the trend towards lower tariffs became general in the mid-1980s, the region's share of world trade has not increased. Raw materials still predominate among Latin American exports. Industry's economic importance within the region has declined (Table 2.2; Bulmer-Thomas 1994: 334–8, 383–7, 400–1). The recent weakness of Latin American manufacturing is due partly to persistent macro-economic instability. The austerity measures required to meet debt charges have depressed the home market. Governments cannot afford to provide technical support, or invest in essential infrastructure, such as telecommunications and electric power generation. But sudden exposure to foreign industrial competition has made these difficulties worse, by putting many firms out of business, or so weakening their finances that they cannot afford necessary improvements (Williamson 1990: 320; Green 1995: 77–9). Neoliberals cite Chile, the strongest Latin American economy by the early 1990s, and the pioneer of tariff liberalization, as evidence that the strategy does eventually work. They argue that some time must pass, perhaps longer than originally expected, before the necessary improvements in economic structure and business attitudes are achieved, after decades of ISI. Yet Chile may not provide a feasible model for the rest of Latin America. The country's recent economic revival depends heavily on natural resource advantages in exporting certain 'non-traditional' commodities (fruit, wine, timber, fish) to supplement copper, the established staple (Green 1995: 216–17; Collins and Lear 1995). Also, Chile's distinctive political history has made possible exceptionally far-reaching institutional reforms (Chapters 4, 5 and 8).

Most of the East Asian NICs relaxed tariff protection gradually, easing firms' adjustment to international competition. The needs of manufacturers that required imported inputs for export production were first met by selective duty rebates rather than comprehensive liberalization. Infant industries had a protected home market base from which to develop export sales, while being encouraged to raise efficiency towards international standards by government assistance, and by warnings that tariffs would be lowered in the future (Hewitt *et al.* 1992: 110–11, 177).

Returning to Latin America, Chile's post-1973 military rulers undertook a rapid tariff liberalization because they believed that ISI had fostered collectivist mentalities and allowed a communist-led labour movement, nurtured by an overprotected manufacturing sector, to gain power. It was felt necessary to cleanse society of these influences as quickly as possible. Military regimes in the other Southern Cone countries took a similar course, influenced by a similar doctrinaire revulsion to the threat from the radical left (Frieden 1991: 155–8, 206–11). Since 1982 foreign creditors, mobilized through the Washington consensus, have had more influence on Latin American policy. They argue that liberalization should be rapid, to ensure that the process is sustained. The vested interests associated with the old protective system must be allowed no time to regroup and reassert themselves (World Bank 1987: 100, 108–10). Cases are cited where firms established under ISI lobbied to obstruct attempts at piecemeal reform during the 1960s and 1970s (Morawetz 1981: 98–9; Frieden 1991: 196).

Perhaps Latin American political circumstances made it necessary to cut tariffs quickly, but the approach entailed economic costs. In South Korea and Taiwan, on the other hand, trade liberalization occurred at a more measured pace, determined by pragmatic national administrators, who could judge accurately the competitive potential of the industries under their supervision (Lin 1989: 67–72).

FINANCIAL LIBERALIZATION AND INTERNATIONAL CAPITAL FLOWS

Latin America has been adversely affected by premature, over-rapid financial liberalization. In the late 1970s the Southern Cone countries, following the neoliberal agenda, gave banks and private individuals more freedom to convert funds between national and foreign currencies. The higher interest rates permitted under the new financial regime soon attracted large inflows of foreign money, much of it channelled through the deregulated banking systems as credit for buying foreign cars, cameras, watches, and other luxury imported goods, to which consumers had been given access by tariff liberalization. At the same time the capital inflows raised REERs and made exporting more difficult. Large trade deficits resulted. Lending booms of this type were unsustainable, because they did not finance productive investment. But according to the raw neoliberalism that influenced Southern Cone policy, private-sector debtors and creditors should be 'rational', capable of judging transactions for themselves, without detailed official oversight. Nevertheless, as the situation became more precarious, governments intervened. They borrowed abroad to support national currencies at increasingly overvalued rates, with the aim of controlling inflation and preventing a banking collapse, while private wealth holders, fearing an imminent devaluation, converted assets into foreign currency and transferred them abroad. In the early 1980s large-scale capital flight also occurred from Mexico, where the long border with the US made financial controls difficult to enforce, and from Venezuela, relatively 'open' because of its oil industry. By 1983 about US $160 billion of privately owned Latin American flight capital was held abroad, mainly in First World bank accounts (Bulmer-Thomas 1994: 338–41; Frieden 1991: 158–73, 212–15; Banuri 1991: 18, 47–9, 75, 88–9).

More recently Latin America has again experienced volatile international capital movements. In 1991 a large financial inflow, much of it repatriated flight capital, resumed for the first time since 1982, encouraged by the apparent success of a US-backed scheme for debt relief (Chapter 3), falling US interest rates, and the feeling that neoliberal reforms were beginning to solve Latin America's economic problems. The main vehicle for investment was not bank lending, as in the 1970s, but the sale of Latin American bonds and shares, often in newly privatized businesses. The recession which affected the developed countries in the early 1990s helped to stimulate enthusiasm for the high returns offered by 'emerging' stockmarkets. Between 1991 and 1993 Mexico was the leading Third World recipient of foreign capital, attracting US $75 billion. The influx raised the REER and held back exports. Then in January 1994 US interest rates began to rise once more. At the same time a rural uprising broke out unexpectedly in the southern Mexican state of Chiapas, evoking memories of the country's violent past. (The Chiapas rebels called themselves Zapatistas, after a peasant leader of the 1910–20 revolution.) A few weeks later investors were further alarmed by the assassination of the governing party's presidential election candidate, and they began selling off Mexican securities on a massive scale. The central bank's foreign currency reserves fell by $25 billion in the course of the year, forcing a devaluation and austerity measures that once more put the country into deep recession (Green 1995: 85–7). The Mexican crisis has shaken other Latin American countries, especially Argentina, where in 1991 the currency was made fully convertible, to limit inflation, attract money from abroad, and ensure the success of a privatization programme. However, the effects have been limited in Colombia and Chile, which both maintain quite stringent financial controls (reintroduced by Chile after 1982).

Doctrinaire neoliberals claim that vulnerability to financial crises is determined above all by underlying economic conditions. In practice, it is alleged, capital controls can be evaded. International money flows represent the means by which wealth holders pass judgement on the 'soundness' of national policy. These arguments seem dubious, or at least overstated. For example, Brazil operated controls and suffered little capital flight in the early 1980s, despite the country's serious inflation and balance of payments problems (Hewitt *et al.* 1992: 184–6). Experience shows that money markets are often highly erratic, and that developing countries should maintain capital controls to limit speculative excess, certainly until the domestic financial situation is stabilized. The East Asian NICs' approach to financial deregulation has been very cautious.

CONCLUSION

Latin American development strategies remained too inward looking for too long, but the policy changes correcting this introversion, begun in the Southern Cone during the 1970s, and continued more widely after 1982, were excessively abrupt. While export-based manufacturing growth has proved more efficient than ISI, in other respects neoliberal prescriptions involve a misreading of the East Asian experience, and they are unlikely to foster a strong economic recovery.

It is clear that some Latin American weaknesses are above all domestic in origin, for example the problems of inflation and REER instability, or the maladministration of industrial policy. However, other difficulties may perhaps be seen more as the result of unfavourable international circumstances. The immediate cause of the 1982 debt crisis was the sudden rise in interest rates generated by the developed countries' turn to 'monetarist' economics. Subsequently Latin America was heavily burdened by the service charges on its foreign loans, and indebtedness has also required the imposition of unhelpful neoliberal measures. The next two chapters will consider further the role of internal and external forces as influences on the region.

3   Latin America and the wider world

Chapter 1 noted how the East Asian NICs' economic success has called into question dependency theory, and its argument that Latin American problems result largely from the effects of First World capitalism. Nevertheless, while the dependency perspective may not be equally valid for all developing regions, does it still offer useful insights on Latin America? Have international circumstances here been particularly unfavourable, perhaps more so than in East Asia?

Latin America is part of the Western Hemisphere, lying at a distance from Europe, Africa, and Asia, but close to the United States, for most of the twentieth century the world's richest and most powerful country. Possible advantages of this location include ready access to the US as an export market and as a source of investment. Latin America escaped the destructive effects of the two world wars. Spending by North American tourists, and the earnings of emigrant workers in the US, have made important contributions to the national income of Mexico and other Caribbean basin countries. However, US pre-eminence may also have been unhelpful to Latin America in various ways. This chapter considers whether the US has had seriously damaging effects on its southern neighbours, through political intervention, through economic penetration by MNCs (most of them US-based), through the financial leverage associated with the debt crisis, and through the stimulus given by North American demand to the Latin American narcotics industry. It is argued here that since 1945 Latin America as a whole has not in fact been handicapped to any great extent by unfavourable external circumstances. The harm caused by the US in the region is often exaggerated.

US INTERVENTION

US claims to a special leadership role in the Western Hemisphere began with the declaration by President Monroe in 1823, following Latin American independence, that the Americas should not be subject to any new colonization from outside the region. The enormous growth of US economic strength during the later nineteenth century made the country more aggressive. The Monroe doctrine was extended under Theodore Roosevelt's presidency (1901–8) to justify armed 'police' intervention in neighbouring states, when their chronic disorder and failure to pay foreign creditors might provoke interference by European powers. However, by the 1920s account had to be taken of growing Latin American nationalist feeling, itself partly a response to overbearing US behaviour. In the 1930s economic depression checked US assertiveness, and President Franklin Roosevelt's 'good neighbor' policy repudiated interventionism. Then World War II revived the US economy, restored national self-confidence, and made the country determined to take a leading international role. By 1945 the US accounted for more than half the world's industrial production, completely eclipsing former European rivals in Latin American investment and trade (Keen 1996: 522–36).

From the later 1940s the main US foreign policy concern became the threat of communist expansion posed by the Soviet Union and China. Western Europe and East Asia, the front lines in the cold war, were to be held by direct US military engagement, combined with generous support for economic reconstruction. (US aid amounted to 5–10 per cent of national income in Taiwan and South Korea during the 1950s.) The Western Hemisphere was less immediately at risk and could be secured more cheaply, through a system of US-led treaties. The US urged its Latin American allies to sever diplomatic ties with the Soviet Union and outlaw local communist parties. Washington feared that communist-inspired labour unrest within the region threatened the supply of strategic raw materials. Very little economic aid was forthcoming, but the US supplied instruction and equipment to Latin American militaries. The onset of the cold war apparently checked the progressive political tendencies that had affected Latin America in the mid-1940s, inspired by the US–Soviet alliance against Nazi Germany. From 1948 a number of recently established reforming governments were overthrown by the armed forces, with US approval or acquiescence (Bethell and Roxborough 1992). The swing to the right in US domestic politics induced by the cold war led to the election of the Republican Dwight Eisenhower as president. Several important posts in his administration (1953–60) were held by men drawn from business. Their hostility to Latin America's government-backed ISI provided a further reason for withholding economic assistance (Skidmore and Smith 1997: 372–80).

The US modified its policy when the 1959 Cuban Revolution showed that a corrupt, immobile dictatorship gave inadequate protection against communism. President Kennedy's Alliance for Progress offered finance for economic development and social reform, but this was combined with programmes to strengthen Latin American counter-insurgency capabilities. 'National security doctrine', emphasizing the armed forces' role as guardians against international communism, gave ideological support to a new wave of military coups, most notably in Brazil (1964) and Argentina (1962, 1966). Later the US worked actively to destabilize the Marxist-influenced government of Salvador Allende in Chile. Therefore, it is argued, US cold war anxieties may have reinforced Latin American authoritarianism, thwarted efforts to put development on a more secure, equitable basis, and aggravated political instability (Smith 1994; Sheahan 1987: 340–54; Keen 1996: 536–55).

> The worst side of external pressure is not the operation of the world economy in general but the quite specific intervention of the United States. At the same time as the United States provides real help in many contexts it has constituted a persistent force on the side of repression whenever any signs of communist influence can be detected.
>
> (Sheahan 1987: 361)

Nevertheless, the significance of the US in Latin American politics should not be exaggerated. First, we must distinguish between the small Caribbean basin republics, which have been highly susceptible to external pressure, and the rest of Latin America (including Mexico), which has enjoyed much greater autonomy. In the Caribbean and Central America the US has often prevailed simply by bringing overwhelming strength to bear against limited opposition, as with the seizure of the territory required for building the Panama Canal (1903). US troops administered Nicaragua (1912–33), Haiti (1915–34), the Dominican Republic (1916–24), and Cuba (1917–23). Subsequently US-trained National Guards sustained notorious client dictators: the Somozas in Nicaragua, and Rafael Trujillo in the Dominican Republic (Rouquié 1987: 120–8). The US backed the invasion that brought down Guatemala's reformist government in 1954 (Gleijeses 1991). US forces have been deployed more recently in Grenada (1983) and Panama (1989).

However, such direct action was not feasible elsewhere. Any political interference attempted in the larger republics had to be undertaken through local proxies. Some authors emphasize the close ties cultivated by the US with Latin America's armed forces, through military aid, and through training programmes that inculcated a cold war, anti-communist mentality (Keen 1996: 573). The difficulty here is that fear of communism was already firmly established by the 1930s in Latin American upper-class and military circles, without any encouragement from the US. So arguably the 1944–6 'social democratic opening' should be seen as anomalous, an expression of the euphoria generated by the wartime US–Soviet alliance, while the subsequent reaction was a return to 'routine politics' (Bethell 1994b: 137, 175–80, 328–9). In any case, despite the 'conservative consolidation' of the early cold war period, during the 1950s elected civilian regimes were the most common Latin American government type, and populist leaders had a substantial influence. The more widespread shift in the 1960s to military dictatorship was provoked mainly by domestic influences, though the US and its cold war concerns may have played a secondary, conditioning role (Chapter 4; Rouquié 1987: 117–50).

Apart from the possibilities for military intervention, the US has also had a powerful economic hold over its smaller neighbours. Until the 1959 revolution Cuba was kept in a state of abject and demoralized subordination by the island's reliance on the US as a market for its sugar. Some of the Central American republics depended heavily on the US-controlled banana trade. But, once again, the position elsewhere was quite different. Strong nationalist feelings had developed and they were still asserted even if government became more socially conservative. For example, Chile's swing to the right after 1947 was accompanied by further increases in the tax rates imposed on US copper mining companies (Moran 1974: 24, 176–9). The Eisenhower administration may have been unsympathetic to state enterprise and ISI, but Washington never seriously considered retaliating with its own tariff measures against protectionism in the larger republics.

It is not clear that US economic assistance gave South Korea and Taiwan a significant advantage over Latin America. Both countries had suffered extensive war damage, and both were obliged to maintain large armed forces against threatening communist neighbours. Some authors imply that the US exercised leverage as an aid donor to ensure that South Korea and Taiwan implemented land reforms, and other helpful measures (Green 1995: 181–2; Haggard 1990: 67–70). However, the two countries ignored US advice on other points, for example by maintaining interventionist industrial policies. When substantial US aid did reach Latin America, for Bolivia after its 1952 revolution (Keen 1996: 538), and the region as a whole after 1960, very little was achieved.

Finally, from the mid-1960s various international developments weakened the US position in Latin America. Washington was distracted by the Vietnam War, by the Middle East, and by the pursuit of improved relations with the Soviet Union and China. Cold war tensions eased. The Soviet Union and Cuba worked hard to conciliate Latin American opinion by distancing themselves from strategies of armed revolution. Moscow established or re-established a diplomatic representation in most of the region's capitals. The economic resurgence of Western Europe and Japan provided a commercial counterweight to the US in the Americas.

This changing context gave Latin American governments extra room for manoeuvre. Many of the military rulers that gained power in the later 1960s did not view communism as a serious threat, took a radical 'anti-imperialist' line, and launched ambitious schemes for social reform. Panama's General Torrijos pursued the issue of US sovereignty over the Canal Zone. In Peru General Velasco's administration (1968–75) expropriated most of the large landed estates. It also nationalized several important US enterprises, without offering satisfactory compensation. Washington withheld official aid and credits, but Peru defeated the financial blockade by securing Eurocurrency loans from commercial banks. Foreign capital was obtained for an ambitious new copper mining project on the strength of sales prospects in Europe and Japan. Armaments were supplied by the Soviet Union. The severe difficulties eventually encountered by Peru's reformist experiment resulted more from national mismanagement than from external pressures (Sheahan 1987: 257–65; Stallings 1987: 271–9; Rouquié 1987: 312–18).

The US showed intense hostility to Salvador Allende's government in Chile, because of his Marxist orientation. However, despite allegations made at the time, it is doubtful whether the US Central Intelligence Agency's schemes for economic sabotage and political destabilization made a decisive contribution to the overthrow of Allende by the military in 1973 (Martz 1988: 167–8). The other authoritarian coups of the period, in Uruguay (1973) and Argentina (1976), certainly occurred without significant US involvement.

During his term of office (1977–80) President Carter tried to give a new high-principled, moral tone to US foreign relations. Military equipment and economic aid were withheld from Latin American governments which had unsatisfactory records on human rights. Carter negotiated the eventual hand-over of the Canal Zone to

Panama. He ensured a democractic transfer of power in the Dominican Republic. He may have deterred an army coup in Bolivia. The withdrawal of US support from Somoza assisted the Sandinista victory in Nicaragua. But Carter's approach achieved little in the larger republics. Brazil and Argentina responded to his embargo on military supplies by purchasing weaponry elsewhere, and by promoting their own armaments industries. When denied US nuclear technology they turned to Germany instead. The Soviet Union provided shipments of uranium. In 1960, 75 per cent of Latin America's arms imports came from the US. That figure had fallen to 20 per cent by 1970 and to 7 per cent by 1980 (Smith 1994: 11).

The Reagan administration began in 1981 by rededicating national policy to a world-wide struggle against Soviet communism, and showed a renewed warmth towards Latin America's dictatorships as useful allies. However, once again the course of Latin American events failed to match US preferences, and a strong regional movement away from authoritarian rule soon began, initiated by the downfall of the Argentine military junta after the defeat of its attempt to occupy the Falkland Islands in 1982, an adventure undertaken against strong US advice. The debt crisis then reinforced the trend, which Washington felt obliged to accept with good grace. So the promotion of democracy became a major rhetorical theme of Ronald Reagan's presidency, partly as justification for his obsessive campaign against Nicaragua's Sandinista government, and during the later 1980s this new policy helped to oust some of Latin America's few remaining dictators (Carothers 1991).

MULTINATIONAL CORPORATE INVESTMENT

Large foreign firms have taken a conspicuous role in Latin America. Originally foreign investment was concentrated in primary export sectors (for example, sugar plantations, or mining), and in infrastructure (railways, electricity supply, telephone services). After 1945 it focused more on manufacturing industry. By the 1970s multinational corporations accounted for about 30 per cent of Latin American manufacturing output. For the East Asian NICs the corresponding figure was only about 10 per cent in South Korea, Taiwan, and Hong Kong, though the proportion reached 50 per cent in Singapore. Most MNC investment in Latin America has come from the US, but since the 1960s European and Japanese firms have become more prominent.

It is suggested that MNC penetration has had many harmful consequences for Latin America. The MNCs' control of advanced technology allows them to exercise monopoly power, and take out large profits, at the expense of the host countries' balance of payments (Skidmore and Smith 1997: 387–8). The MNCs have been reluctant to produce for export from their Latin American operations, in competition with parent companies' plants elsewhere. The MNCs tend to operate as isolated enclaves, making little use of local suppliers, and preferring capital-intensive methods that require only a small workforce. In certain sectors, for example the pharmaceutical industry, MNCs acquired locally owned firms which had quite high levels of technical expertise. The subsidiaries then gave up research and development work, to concentrate instead on routine manufacturing. Much MNC investment is dedicated to the supply of consumer durables, such as motor cars, for the upper and middle classes. The MNCs' advertising campaigns to promote affluent developed country lifestyles may have encouraged spending and limited personal savings (Bennett and Sharpe 1985).

Countries which became dependent on foreign investment had to offer the reassurance of a 'safe' business climate, with a docile, low-cost labour force, secured by political repression. The regional trend towards military dictatorship after 1960 has been explained partly in these terms. During the early stages of ISI, the argument runs, Latin American manufacturing was mainly controlled by indigenous entrepreneurs, and was dedicated to supplying a mass market with relatively simple products (for example clothing, shoes, furniture). Businessmen therefore benefited from high wages to ensure a widely distributed purchasing power, and favoured democratic, populist regimes. However, the MNCs' entry shifted industry towards luxury durables, and required a greater income concentration in the hands of the rich to ensure a sufficient demand (Keen 1996: 563; Evans 1979: 29–38).

The lobbying power of large firms in Washington perhaps encouraged US action to prevent Latin American reform. The United Fruit Company's connections with the Eisenhower administration allegedly provoked the 1954 intervention against Guatemala, where the company's banana plantations were under threat. ITT, a US conglomerate, reacted to the expropriation of its Chilean business in the early 1970s by urging action against the Allende government (Keen 1996: 539–42). 'Latin American democracy could have been healthier in the last generation if foreign investment had been ruled out' (Sheahan 1987: 360).

Most of these points are open to question. First, the MNCs on the whole did not force themselves into Latin America. They usually invested as a result of measures designed to attract them by national governments, so any harm that followed can be seen more as the expression of weaknesses internal to the region, rather than as an external imposition. For example, Brazil's MNC-controlled automobile assembly industry was established in the 1950s despite technical studies which showed that the country would have benefited from a greater emphasis on railways. However, railway improvement, or the establishment of a state-owned automobile firm as a 'national champion', required heavy government spending, and the taxes to pay for this could not be raised because of domestic political difficulties (Shapiro 1994: 28–69).

Second, although it is true that during the early years of their Latin American operations in the 1950s and 1960s MNC manufacturing enterprises often did make unreasonably high profits, while failing to purchase local supplies or to share technology, with the passage of time these faults were recognized. As host governments built up the necessary expertise, they bargained more effectively, imposing more stringent rules, concerning import content and other matters, on foreign firms (Bennett and Sharpe 1985). New investments were increasingly confined to joint ventures with local capital, as under Brazil's *tri-pé* system of three-way partnership between MNCs, state enterprises, and private-sector national firms (Evans 1979).

Third, it is unlikely that an ingrained reluctance on the part of the MNCs to export from their subsidiaries has seriously weakened Latin America's balance of payments or aggravated the region's foreign indebtedness. Over the last thirty years competitive pressures have encouraged MNCs to supply much of their global business from operations in developing countries, where labour costs are relatively low. MNC branch plants in East Asia have been export-oriented, useful earners of foreign exchange for their host countries, despite profit remittances. It is local circumstances – overvalued currencies, political uncertainty, poor infrastructure – that have done most to prevent the MNCs from playing a similar role in Latin America. Even here MNC manufacturing enterprises had come by the 1970s to export a greater proportion of their output than did national firms (Haggard 1990: 218).

Finally, allegations that the MNCs have had more generally harmful effects on Latin American society and politics are also problematic. Latin American elites developed an enthusiasm for motor cars and the other elements of developed country consumerism before corporate advertising became a major influence within the region (Bennett and Sharpe 1985: 99–101; Shapiro 1994: 30–2). The main causes of income inequality are to be found in nationally determined patterns of landownership, industrial structure, and social welfare provision (Chapters 4 and 5). The MNCs cannot be held primarily responsible for the US government's anti-reformist interventions in Latin America. Several studies show that since 1945 strategic security objectives have taken precedence over business interests in determining US foreign policy. For example, it now seems that, contrary to allegations made at the time, the US action against Guatemala in 1954 was provoked by well-founded reports of communist infiltration, and not by the United Fruit Company's lobbying (Gleijeses 1991: 361–6). Indeed, many US firms doing business in Latin America have been reluctant to seek help from Washington, judging that this would increase nationalist hostility. A provocative stance of the type taken by ITT against the Allende government in Chile has come to be seen as outdated and unhelpful (Martz 1988: 45–52; Lowenthal 1991: 142–73).

FOREIGN DEBT AND INTERNATIONAL FINANCE

In recent years Latin America's relations with the wider world have been dominated by the issue of debt. Following its rapid growth during the 1970s, international bank lending to the region fell sharply after 1982. Inflows of new money were exceeded by outflows of interest payments. Between 1983 and 1990 the annual resource transfer from Latin America to foreign creditors averaged about 3 per cent of regional output, a severe drain (Bethell 1994a: 245). In 1991 a net capital inflow resumed, but this was curtailed by the Mexican crisis of 1994 (Chapter 2). In 1995 debt charges still absorbed nearly half Latin America's export earnings (IMF 1996: 39).

Quite clearly indebtedness has become one of Latin America's most serious problems. Chapter 2 presented it as a symptom or consequence of more fundamental internal weaknesses, rather than as an external imposition. Because Latin American export earnings did not meet import requirements, foreign borrowing had to cover balance of payments deficits. However, Latin America may also have been put at a disadvantage by the workings of international money markets.

During the 1970s First World banks competed with each other to attract the funds accumulated by the Middle East oil producers following the OPEC price increases. Profitable uses then had to be found for the petrodollar deposits, and with the developed countries in recession, Latin America seemed one of the most promising outlets. Its governments were pursuing plausible development plans. Natural resource abundance gave the region good prospects as a source of raw materials exports, and it was widely assumed at the time that commodity prices would rise over the long term. International banks were already well established in Latin America, and they hoped to enlarge their presence. So, it is suggested, First World bankers actively 'pushed' loans onto Latin American borrowers. The fall in interest rates charged, and various other indicators, give some support to the thesis that the growth of lending was driven by supply-side influences (Stallings 1987: 161–85; Green 1991: 73–4; Frieden 1991: 53–66). Then in the early 1980s Latin America suffered the double blow of a sudden rise in interest rates, when the US and British governments adopted monetarist economic policies, combined with depressed export demand for raw materials. Mexico's difficulties were most acute, because it was so reliant on oil sales and vulnerable to capital flight, undermining lenders' confidence in Latin America as a whole through a 'contagion effect' (Banuri 1991: 22). The debt crisis may therefore be said to have resulted largely from the operation of external forces .

However, these arguments are open to a number of objections. Some resource-abundant Asian countries, for example Malaysia and Indonesia, benefited from the 1970s commodities boom while showing restraint as borrowers. Within Latin America there is the case of Colombia, where a distinctive pattern of domestic politics (Chapter 4) ensured financial prudence, and the foreign debt remained quite modest. The most authoritative analysis of the subject concludes that over the region as a whole, foreign banks' desire to extend credit was fully matched by Latin Americans' wish to borrow. The debt build-up resulted from the interplay of supply and demand forces. 'Despite some revisionist claims lenders were rarely "forcing" money on reluctant borrowers . . . ' (Stallings 1987: 6–7).

After the onset of the debt crisis Latin American policy contrasted with the course followed half a century earlier, when the 1929 Wall Street crash led to a similar breakdown of international lending. In the 1930s most Latin American countries soon defaulted (stopped payment) on their foreign debt. They became less dependent on exports, and achieved quite rapid economic recovery through inward-looking development (Bulmer-Thomas 1994: 194–237). In the 1980s Latin America tried to honour its debts, began accepting its creditors' advice by turning away from ISI, and suffered a long recession. So why did Latin America not default once again?

The 1980s policy response was different for two reasons: first, by this time national experience had discredited ISI strategies, and second, international circumstances had changed. In the 1930s Latin American foreign debt was held by many thousands of private US and European bondholders. They lacked political influence and their governments, still strongly influenced by *laissez-faire* ideology, did little to discourage Latin American default. However, in the 1980s most Latin American debt was held by a few major developed country banks, which had become dangerously committed or 'exposed' on their Third World lending. It was feared that defaults might make some of these banks fail, leading to a more widespread economic collapse.

Therefore the US government coordinated agreements for the rescheduling (partial postponement) of debt payments, through negotiations involving creditor banks, the IMF, and other Washington-based agencies (Stallings 1987: 103–5). Debtor countries, dealt with individually on a case-by-case basis, undertook to continue meeting their obligations, thus ensuring the creditor banks' continued solvency. Debtors were induced to accept rescheduling because it offered the prospect of further loans as a reward for 'good behaviour', though in fact additional finance did not materialize on any large scale for several years. But a coercive element was also involved through the creditors' common front, organized under US leadership. The US anti-trust legislation, intended to deter collusion between firms, was not applied against banks involved with the problem of Third World debt. So default by a Latin American country might be punished with complete exclusion from international money markets, even for the short-term trade credits used to finance current import/export business (Bulmer-Thomas 1994: 370). Other possible sanctions included the confiscation of assets held abroad as flight capital.

Yet while the creditors' cartel exercised powerful leverage over debtor countries, there were some mitigating features. Washington opinion recognized that a prolonged Latin American economic downturn might have dangerous ramifications, perhaps causing political upheavals in Mexico and further south, which would enlarge the flow of illegal migrants to the US. There was also concern for Mexico's stability as a source of oil. Thus the feeling prevailed that creditors should not press their negotiating advantage too hard, and debtor countries should be allowed to earn the export revenue which they needed to satisfy the terms of rescheduling agreements. The Reagan administration successfully resisted congressional demands that the access of foreign goods to the US market be restricted (Martz 1988: 126), even though domestic protectionist pressures had become very strong, because of the competitive weakness shown by several national industries. The commitment of key policy makers to maintaining relatively free trade derived from neoliberal economic theory, and from their reading of economic history. The 1930s depression, it was believed, had been made worse by the general resort to 'beggar my neighbour' protective tariffs. So during the 1980s the US ran large trade deficits, provided a buoyant market for imports, and ensured the continued growth of world trade.

South Korea benefited from these favourable circumstances to increase its exports and maintain rapid economic growth, despite suffering a large net resource outflow through service charges on outstanding loans. However, Latin America as a whole failed to respond in the same way, because of national weaknesses in economic structure and management. Chile is an exception on this point. In 1982 the country had one of the region's heaviest debt burdens, yet in 1984 the country began an export-led recovery that has been sustained ever since, backed by unusually effective policy implementation (Chapter 4; Hojman 1993).

As it became clear that most debtor countries were not solving their problems through a strengthened export performance, Washington began to shift away from its original strategy centred around rescheduling agreements. In 1985 US Treasury Secretary James Baker made proposals for a large increase of new international lending. The 'Baker plan' was abortive, because developed country banks withheld support, but a subsequent initiative by Treasury Secretary Nicholas Brady proved more effective. The 1989 'Brady plan' offered indebted countries the partial forgiveness or writing down of their liabilities, in return for commitments to policy reform along neoliberal lines.

The new approach was possible because since 1982 the major international banks' financial position had been improved through the accumulation of profits and the issue of new shares. Having established a stronger capital base, the banks could write off some of their Third World debt without becoming insolvent. First World governments allowed loan-loss provisions to be set against tax liabilities, in effect subsidizing debt relief (Bulmer-Thomas 1994: 373–7). The Brady plan laid the basis for the resumption of large-scale capital inflows to Latin America from 1991, although they were checked by the difficulties that affected Mexico in 1994–5. As noticed earlier, the crisis was caused partly by Mexico's premature financial liberalization, undertaken at the urging of foreign creditors (Chapter 2), but domestic factors were significant too. The Chiapas uprising came as a response to rural poverty. Political uncertainties were heightened by the aura of corruption and criminality, probably involving the narcotics trade, that surrounds the *PRI*, the national governing party. And outside assistance was made available to help retrieve the situation. In 1995 Washington coordinated a US $50 billion international rescue package for the Mexican currency (Green 1995: 85–7). Once again self-interest impelled the US to support its southern neighbours.

THE NARCOTICS TRADE

The last three decades have seen the expansion of a Latin American-based narcotics industry, stimulated by demand from the US as the primary market, though major deliveries are now also reaching Europe. Cultivation of the opium poppy for processing into heroin was established on a large scale in Mexico during the early 1970s, after Middle Eastern heroin consignments to North America via the 'French connection' had been disrupted by police action. Mexico also became a source of marijuana for the US. Then in the later 1970s the lead was taken by cocaine, manufactured from the leaves of the coca bush, a plant indigenous to the eastern foothills of the South American Andes. The chewing of coca leaves is traditional in the Andean region, serving the Indian poor as a mild narcotic that helps them to endure hunger, thirst, and hard labour. However, consumption was static or declining until the US generated an explosive growth in demand for the more powerful derivative.

At first the extension of coca growing occurred in eastern Peru and Bolivia, while cocaine was processed for export in Colombia, already an important supplier of marijuana to the US. As a response the US sought Latin American cooperation in a succession of anti-drugs campaigns. Washington gave logistic aid and training to programmes aimed at interdicting supply routes, pursuing individual traffickers, destroying production at source, and encouraging economic alternatives. US troops have been deployed on anti-drugs missions in Peru and Bolivia. So far these measures have had little success. The Colombian security forces have killed or captured some of the country's most notorious drugs barons, associated in the so-called Medellín 'cartel', but other trafficking groups centred on the city of Cali have survived relatively unscathed. Coca cultivation has been introduced to Colombia. Refining laboratories have been established in Peru and Bolivia. Heroin production has developed as a complementary activity. New marketing networks through Central America have supplemented the original Colombian operations. Mexican supply routes are now reckoned to account for about three-quarters of the cocaine reaching the US, along with considerable quantities of heroin and marijuana. The large population of Mexican immigrants in the US provides convenient distribution channels. The drugs industry, aided by new communications technologies and the recent acceleration in world-wide economic integration, has become so sophisticated and so pervasive as to be apparently beyond police control (Tullis 1995).

Why have attempts at curbing the Latin American narcotics trade had so little effect? Obviously the continuing strength of foreign demand must take part of the blame. Latin Americans argue that the drugs boom results primarily from US social ills, and therefore that the US government should pay more attention to curbing consumption. Instead, Washington has given priority to its intrusive supply control programmes, stirring up nationalist feelings within Latin America and discouraging local cooperation against narcotics. Bolivian coca growers, organized in militant peasant unions that play on general public distaste for US interference with a 'traditional' activity, have thwarted anti-drugs measures with road blocks and mass demonstrations (Tullis 1995: 72, 102). In 1989 the US invaded Panama to seize the dictator General Noriega and bring him to trial on drug-trafficking charges before a Florida court. However, this is another case of the US acting against a small Central American republic in a way that was not feasible elsewhere, and since Noriega's departure Panama's banks remain deeply involved with the laundering of drugs money. Colombia's revised 1991 constitution prohibits the extradition of nationals to stand trial abroad. Furthermore, other foreign policy objectives have compromised US action against Latin American narcotics. The issue has been subordinated in Washington's recent dealings with Mexico to the overriding priority of securing that country's political and economic stability through neoliberal reforms. Agents of the Reagan administration employed drugs traffickers as secret intermediaries to supply the Contra guerrillas fighting the Sandinistas in Nicaragua.

However, the strength of the drugs economy is also a consequence of Latin America's own agrarian inequality and development failure. Cultivation and processing are carried on with a good chance of escaping detection in the region's under-policed frontier zones, where settlement has been promoted as part of misconceived ISI strategies (Chapter 7). Coca growers have responded to eradication drives by moving to more remote parts of Amazonia. Marijuana and opium poppies are grown in deep ravines, to escape aerial surveillance and herbicide spraying. Coca bushes are easy to raise, ideal for farmers with limited capital and skills, such as the Bolivian ex-miners displaced by the collapse of the country's tin industry during the 1980s. Maladministered schemes to promote alternative crops – coffee, pine-apples, bananas – have left peasants without the necessary technical advice, inputs, or access to markets. While coca bushes will flourish on infertile hillsides, legitimate crops require better quality land, from which poor settlers have commonly been excluded by their inability to bribe the officials responsible for its allocation (Morales 1989: 57).

In Peru during the 1980s the radical *Sendero Luminoso* guerrilla movement, nurtured by acute rural poverty, gave protection to coca growing as a source of funds and as an 'anti-imperialist' alignment. There were five separate enforcement agencies charged with combating the drugs industry, all of them out of government control and in lucrative collusion with the traffickers (Morales 1989: xix). It was felt that the army in particular had to be allowed opportunities for money making, as a distraction from politics and an insurance against another military coup. Experience elsewhere shows that narcotics can be curbed if social conditions are more favourable. For example, Turkey has had some success in stopping opium-poppy cultivation, helped by strong central administration and relatively equal landownership.

What have been the consequences of the drugs trade for Latin America? The business might perhaps be seen as useful to the region, providing an unusually buoyant source of export revenue. However, studies of the subject put most emphasis on the harm done (Morales 1989; Tullis 1995). Addiction has become more widespread in producer countries. It is suggested that foreign currency earnings from narcotics have put upward pressure on inflation and real exchange rates, weakening legitimate exports, which are also at risk from the trade sanctions threatened by the US against countries deemed to be insufficiently vigorous allies in the war on drugs (Sheahan 1987: 284). Coca growing, subject to displacement by eradication drives, is a cause of deforestation. Soil and rivers have been poisoned by the sulphuric acid and other chemical wastes from processing sites. Above all, drug trafficking has further weakened state power by aggravating criminality, violence, and political corruption. The large profits involved allow traffickers to subvert judges and enforcement agencies with lavish bribes.

Nevertheless, the damaging effects of the drugs trade should not be exaggerated. Despite its widening ramifications, the business is still heavily concentrated on a few countries (Colombia, Peru, Bolivia, Mexico), where in each case it was reckoned by the mid-1990s to account for about 3–5 per cent of national income and a fifth of export earnings. Coca only grows well in certain parts of Amazonia. There has been some increase in local narcotics consumption, though so far on a rather modest scale by US standards. Alcohol abuse remains a much more serious Latin American problem (Tullis 1995: 49–54). In aggregate terms drugs are extremely lucrative. By the late 1980s annual sales of cocaine were estimated at $20 billion, putting it in second place after oil among the most valuable international commodity trades (Green 1991: 6, 18–19). However, distributors in the developed countries take much of the revenue. There is no clear evidence that drugs income returning to Latin America has substantially affected inflation or the competitiveness of legitimate exports. Colombia, to which these suggestions are most commonly applied, has been increasing its legal exports over the last twenty years at a more rapid rate than any other Latin American country. During the 1980s there was certainly a growth in drugs-related crime, especially in Colombia, where the Medellín traffickers waged open war on the state through campaigns of bombing and assassination. But Colombian society was already exceptionally lawless. Furthermore, the Medellín cartel's excesses provoked government counterattacks which eliminated the cartel's main figures in the early 1990s. Leadership of the drugs trade thus passed to the Cali dealers, who prefer to operate more discreetly, by infiltrating the political process, and assimilating into mainstream business (Tullis 1995: 66–70). In Peru the government has had some notable recent successes against *Sendero Luminoso*, despite the support which the movement got from the drugs business. It may be that Latin America's narcotics-related organized crime is establishing a less disruptive relationship with society at large, of the type long familiar in the US, Italy, and parts of East Asia.

CONCLUSION

External forces have not been the primary cause of Latin America's difficulties since 1945. US intervention and influence have only had decisive effects in some of the smaller Caribbean basin republics. Elsewhere the relationship between changing US official attitudes and the course of Latin American politics has been rather loose. Washington cannot bear much responsibility for the deficiencies of the region's governments. The criticisms levelled against MNC investment by dependency theory are unconvincing. The unhelpful features of such business penetration, for example the premature emphasis on consumer durables, came for the most part as the result of policy choices determined within Latin America. The accumulation of foreign debt also resulted mainly from national policies, and international creditors have exercised some restraint in enforcing their claims. The Latin American drugs trade has been fostered by chronic rural poverty. Therefore it seems that the fundamental obstacles to achieving sustained development in Latin America over the last half century should be sought in the region's own social and political characteristics. These are the concern of the next chapter.

4   Society and politics

Latin American society in 1945 was still mainly rural and agricultur-
ally based, with about 30 per cent of the population living in towns, a
figure that had risen to 70 per cent by the 1990s. Compared with the
larger East Asian NICs, Latin American urbanization levels were
already relatively high in the 1940s, while the subsequent population
shift into cities and out of farming occurred at a slightly less rapid
pace. However, Latin America's most distinctive social feature has
been unusually marked income inequalities between rich and poor
(Table 4.1). During the oligarchical period such disparities were based
on elite control over government, large landed estates, and coercive
labour recruitment methods. This chapter first discusses why Latin
American inequality has persisted, or perhaps even grown wider,
despite the decline of agriculture's relative economic importance and
some enlargement of political participation. We then examine the
features of Latin American politics that have caused endemic government weakness and instability.

Table 4.1 Income inequality, circa 1988 (% share of household income, by
             percentile group of households)

		Poorest 20%	Richest 10%
Argentina	1989	4.1	35.9
Brazil	1989	2.1	51.3
Mexico	1984	4.1	39.5
South Korea	1988	7.4	27.6
United Kingdom	1988	4.6	27.8
United States	1985	4.7	25.0

Source World Bank 1995: 221

RURAL SOCIETY

The distribution of Latin American landownership established by the early twentieth century was grossly unequal. A small minority of large holdings had become overwhelmingly predominant. (For example, in Mexico at the outbreak of the 1910–20 revolution *haciendas* held 90 per cent of the country's farm land.) Individual properties extended over several hundreds or even thousands of acres, occupying the most fertile, well-watered tracts, with the best access to markets. Most of the rural population were either poor peasants, supporting themselves from marginal smallholdings, perhaps supplemented by occasional wage work, or lived on the estates as a resident labour force, often allocated subsistence plots under servile tenancies.

Until the late 1950s this agrarian structure continued essentially unchanged, except for the weakening of the *haciendas* that occurred after revolution in Mexico and Bolivia (1952). Latin American populism denounced the estates as archaic survivals. ECLA analysis claimed that their failure to provide the food required by rapidly growing urban populations was a major cause of inflation. Nevertheless, political circumstances (see below) deterred governments from trying to remedy the maldistribution of landholding until the 1959 Cuban Revolution and growing difficulties with ISI gave the issue a new urgency. During the 1960s and 1970s several agrarian reforms were launched, but they had little or no effect in reducing rural income inequality. Schemes were often targeted against underused estates and 'feudal' practices, so owners could react to the threat of expropriation by adopting more mechanized techniques, evicting labour tenants, and converting them into a casual workforce. Large estates often profited from government efforts to strengthen the balance of payments by technical support and subsidized credit for new export crops: cotton and sugar in Central America, or soya beans as an alternative to coffee in Brazil. In Peru nationalized *haciendas* became producer cooperatives, whose permanent employees benefited at the expense of temporary, 'outside' workers. Elsewhere, as in Chile, land redistribution favoured a restricted middle class of capitalist farmers (Sheahan 1987: 130–54).

Some attempts were made at upgrading peasant agriculture through 'integrated rural development' projects, which relied on intensive, small-scale farming methods and village cooperation. Most programmes of this type failed through mismanagement, underfunding, bureaucratic infighting between rival agencies, and the inferiority of the land at the peasants' disposal. Government agronomists took a patronizing, racially prejudiced attitude towards the people they were assigned to help. (Distinct rural Indian populations, defined by language, dress, and ethnicity, remain in Guatemala, Ecuador, Peru, Bolivia, and parts of Mexico. Many of Brazil's rural poor are of African descent.) Where Indian identity had dissolved into the general *mestizo* culture, the usual case over most of Hispanic America, there was still likely to be a marked lack of sympathy between relatively prosperous, educated, light-skinned *técnicos* and mainly illiterate peasants. Also, small farmers' earnings were held down by price controls on basic foodstuffs imposed for the benefit of urban consumers (Bethell 1994a: 360–85; de Janvry 1981). In contrast, in South Korea and Taiwan the comprehensive agrarian reforms undertaken during the 1950s established egalitarian patterns of landownership, while well-organized government technical support raised farmers' incomes and eliminated rural poverty.

URBANIZATION

Latin America's rural income inequalities have been reproduced in the towns. Between the 1940s and the 1970s the region's urban population grew at an annual average rate of 4–5 per cent (doubling every fifteen to twenty years), with about 40 per cent of the increase coming through migration from rural areas. More recently there has been some decline in the rate of urban growth, and in the contribution made to it by rural emigration. Migrants have been both 'pushed' from the countryside by landlessness, poverty, and underemployment, and 'pulled' to the cities by the attractions of urban life. ISI offered new employment opportunities, together with improved education, health care, and other social provision, all concentrated in the major towns (Gilbert 1994: 23–56).

However, although the number of industrial workers grew quite rapidly, the share of the labour force employed in industry remained relatively low, only about 20–25 per cent on average by the 1980s (compared with 30–40 per cent in the leading East Asian NICs). The difference resulted from Latin America's limited success in developing manufactured exports, and from a premature emphasis within the region on labour-saving technology.

The MNCs may have been one cause of the labour-saving bias (Chapter 3), but the bias was also reinforced by other influences. Managers in both national and foreign-owned firms aimed at high levels of automation to counteract what was perceived as insufficient skill and motivation among factory floor operatives. Employment opportunities were also limited by the improved pay and conditions secured through trade union pressure in the larger establishments. Habits of labour militancy had been introduced to Latin America from Europe and the United States during the early twentieth century. Certain key groups – railwaymen, dockers, and miners, for example – found that their capacity to halt the flow of exports gave them considerable leverage. The first strikes provoked harsh repressive measures, but as time passed more subtle techniques of containment evolved, through officially recognized trade unions, arbitrated pay settlements, minimum wages laws, job security, and social welfare benefits for those workers who had political influence and a significant disruptive potential. Even where trade unions developed under government sponsorship and control, as in Mexico or Brazil, their members' acquiescence was bought at the price of substantially increased labour costs, another inducement for employers to adopt capital-intensive, high-productivity methods (Banuri 1991:171–220; Bethell 1994b: 307–57).

Thus job opportunities in industry were limited, and there was a more rapid growth of employment in the service or 'tertiary' sector. Economic development requires more service workers (shop assistants, teachers, architects, doctors, government functionaries, etc.). However, by East Asian or First World standards, Latin American service sector employment accounts for an unusually high share (about 60 per cent) of the urban labour force. It includes many street vendors, shoeblacks, rubbish collectors, and others in precarious occupations. These elements are commonly described as the informal sector, a rather elastic term, embracing a wide range of low-income workers, either self-employed, or employed by others, for example in the small 'sweat shop' factories that larger firms often use as subcontractors, to evade trade unions, minimum wage laws, and other welfare requirements. The informal sector comprises 25–40 per cent of the labour force in Latin American cities, and has been the main means of livelihood for recent migrants from the countryside.

Immigrant and informal-sector workers commonly show great resilience under adverse conditions. They have not constituted a marginal underclass, demoralized by a fatalistic 'culture of poverty', as anticipated by some observers in the 1950s (Roberts 1995: 158–61, 189–94). Many individuals have progressed to more rewarding occupations, or at least secured education and upward mobility for their children. Most newcomers soon relinquish rural ties and assimilate to city life. Temporary urban residence with alternating, 'circular' migration between town and country, a common habit in Africa and South

Asia, is quite unimportant in Latin America. Nevertheless, even during the period of rapid economic growth up to the early 1980s, the earning capacity of the urban poor was held down by their limited skills, by the limited opportunities for better-paid formal-sector work, and by competition from the continuing influx of rural immigrants. The self-employed were liable to official harassment, especially when operating at or beyond the margins of legality. Small-scale businesses suffered exploitation from their suppliers, and restricted access to credit (Bethell 1994a: 276–7, 299–304; Gilbert 1994: 39–71).

Some neoliberals have suggested that cutting back the tangled mass of corruptly administered regulations which underpin the formal/informal-sector divide would allow small enterprises to flourish and put economic development on a more healthy basis (Gilbert 1994: 71–3). Despite the publicity given to this argument, it has not yet been implemented with any vigour, or yielded any substantial results. Since the onset of the debt crisis, low-grade service activities have multiplied further, as a refuge for people affected by falling real wages, cuts in social spending, and the loss of formal-sector employment. The urban poor have born the main brunt of austerity measures. The upper classes, on the other hand, have fared comparatively well: the high interest yields on financial assets required by stabilization programmes and the investment income from holdings of flight capital have compensated for the decline in business profits (Bethell 1994a: 307–12).

Latin American urban geography reflects and reinforces income inequality. The speed at which urbanization occurred put severe pressure on the housing stock, populist rent control laws discouraged private investors from building accommodation to lease out, and governments proved capable of meeting only a small part of the demand for shelter. Most public-sector housing catered for a privileged minority of state employees. Therefore the urban poor resorted to self-built squatter settlements, usually on land occupied through collective invasions, or through illicit purchases that violated planning regulations. Such 'shanty town' development has come to house 30–60 per cent of the population in Latin America's major cities. Governments eradicated particular squatter settlements, but on the whole tolerated the phenomenon as an apparently low-cost expedient, as a way of securing electoral support, and as a safeguard against social discontent. It was hoped that settlers who built and improved their own houses, sometimes to quite high standards, would be diverted from radical politics (Gilbert 1994: 79–101).

All this contrasts with the East Asian NICs, where squatter settlements are strictly controlled and a large part of the urban population is housed in government schemes. They have been more successful here because of greater state autonomy and administrative efficiency. Also, more of the labour force works in capitalist manufacturing or other formal-sector employment, and thus can meet rent or mortgage payments from a regular wage. Most East Asian public housing projects consist of multi-storey apartment blocks. Therefore the region's major cities are relatively compact, while in Latin America the mass of self-built settlement, rarely more than one or two storeys high, has produced low-density sprawl.

Latin America's pattern of extensive urban growth entails serious economic disadvantages, though some authors have seen it as a convenient, if inequitable, way to make cheap labour available for capitalist employers (Abel and Lewis 1993: 112–13). Much squatter settlement property remains without legal title, and thus unacceptable security for bank loans, another obstacle to informal-sector business success. The provision of water, sewerage, and electricity is costly. Buses rather than rail systems (the more efficient alternative) must serve as the main form of public transport. Labour productivity suffers because of time-consuming, exhausting journeys to work, which average 90 minutes in big Latin American cities, compared with 30–45 minutes in their East Asian counterparts. Reliance on long-distance motor vehicle commuting makes transport costs a considerable item in Latin American urban household budgets, and a politically sensitive issue. Governments have held down fuel prices, and then been forced to raise them under austerity programmes, by eliminating subsidies, or imposing new taxes. Rioting against higher bus fares has disrupted several attempts at economic stabilization (Gilbert 1994: 113–19, 146–9; Ward 1990: 92–113).

POLITICS SINCE THE 1940s: GENERAL TRENDS AND SPECIAL CASES

Each Latin American country has its own distinctive political history. However, the most common pattern followed over the last half century included a phase of competitive electoral democracy, subject to occasional military intervention. The period lasted from the 1940s to the 1960s. Then dissatisfaction with erratic civilian rule made the military take power on a longer-term basis. Military dictatorship gave way to a process of redemocratization in the 1980s.

Some countries do not fit this scheme. In Mexico a single party, the *PRI*, has held power continuously as legatee of the 1910–20 revolution, by reinforcing a populist/nationalist appeal with electoral fraud and pervasive patronage networks. Venezuela was controlled by a succession of military dictators until the late 1950s when, after the fall of General Pérez Jiménez, civilian politicians reached an understanding among themselves to guard against the return of authoritarian rule. Subsequently buoyant tax revenues from the country's oil industry funded the political system. While the presidency alternated between the two main parties, their supporters shared access to employment in the proliferating state bureaucracy. The armed forces were kept content with generous pay and equipment grants. The wider electorate benefited from welfare and development programmes.

Colombia's politics have been shaped by the long ascendancy of two rival parties, the Liberals and the Conservatives. There is a tradition of rural violence, dating back to nineteenth-century conflicts, and fostered by the country's rugged geography. Both Liberals and Conservatives have continued under elite leadership, drawing support from across a wide social range. After an episode of civil war and dictatorship in the 1950s the two parties formed a coalition government which agreed on a pragmatic, moderate approach to development issues. ISI was combined with export promotion, balance of payments deficits were contained, and the foreign debt remained modest (Sheahan 1987: 275–88).

Other special cases include Costa Rica, where a comparatively egalitarian pattern of landownership limited social conflict. Costa Rica abolished its army in 1949, and democracy has survived without interruption ever since. However, old-style landed oligarchies dominated the country's Central American neighbours until the 1970s. In Paraguay, even more backward and 'feudal', the personal autocracy of General Alfredo Stroessner held sway from 1954 to 1989. Cuba's position as the world's largest sugar exporter gave the island a period of relative prosperity in the 1940s, when alternative supply sources were disrupted, followed by economic stagnation when competition resumed. The rigidities of the sugar monoculture, and Cuba's dependence on the US as an export market, prevented development through ISI. Nationalist aspirations were frustrated. The rule of the dictator Batista was marked by cynicism, lethargy, and incompetence, so in 1959 Fidel Castro and his small guerrilla band could sweep to power from their rural base. Castro soon nationalized all US and other foreign investments, committing Cuba to socialism in alliance with the Soviet Union. His regime has survived into the 1990s (Wynia 1990: 287–307).

Through all this variety of detail a common failure to maintain viable development strategies affected every regime type. Electoral competition brought chronic political instability and executive weakness. Despite their attempts at 'autonomy', military dictatorships proved susceptible to vested interests and popular dissatisfaction. In Mexico the *PRI*'s long monopoly of power has made administrative corruption deeply ingrained. Venezuela's arrangements gave an appearance of democratic moderation, but frittered away the country's oil wealth. Colombia's two-party consensus blocked agrarian reform and perpetuated high levels of income inequality. The radical left was pushed into armed opposition, aggravating habits of rural lawlessness, and helping to lay the basis for the country's involvement with the international drugs trade (Chapter 3). In Cuba, socialism brought some gains in general welfare, together with extreme economic inefficiency.

CIVILIAN DEMOCRACIES 1940s–1960s

From the 1940s to the 1960s the larger republics usually had elected civilian regimes. Voting rights were extended to most of the adult population. The landed oligarchies' predominance was a thing of the past, and governments responded to the demands from urban interests by promoting ISI. However, for various reasons the new balance of social forces proved highly unstable, and policy implementation suffered as a result.

First, the big landowners had not been eliminated. They could offer a significant challenge to the urban-based populist movements that gained ground during the period. In their early years populist coalitions brought together affluent business and professional people (often referred to as the bourgeoisie) with the lower middle classes and manual workers. These allies cooperated to end exclusive oligarchical rule, but once that objective had been achieved, they soon found reasons for disagreeing among themselves. Workers sought higher wages and welfare benefits. The bourgeoisie took fright at labour militancy and the threat of redistributive taxation, issues on which common cause could be made with elite landowners. Many landowning families proved adaptable. Their members developed interests in manufacturing, commerce, and banking. They entered the higher levels of government service. Successful businessmen from lower-class or immigrant backgrounds could become assimilated into older forms of wealth through marriage alliances and the purchase of estates. Long-standing Latin American customs of highly personalized social relations, based on clientage and *compadrazgo* (ritual kinship), facilitated the intermingling of landed and urban elites (Cubitt 1995: 103–6, 179–86; Roberts 1995: 60–9; Wynia 1990: 47–56).

One economic result was that much private-sector ISI

manufacturing came under the control of a few closely knit oligopolies, their position reinforced by connections with well-placed state officials. Tariff barriers limited competition from imported goods. Collusion between firms to fix prices and share out government favours limited competition within protected domestic markets. The high levels of business profits that resulted helped to perpetuate extreme income inequality. Industrialists had little need to make their factories more efficient.

Habits of partiality, inefficiency, and corruption in public adminis-tration represented another inheritance from the past, with very damaging consequences after 1945 as state functions were enlarged to implement ISI. Latin American traditions of administrative weakness were first established during the colonial period, when both the Spanish and Portuguese monarchies failed to maintain effective control of their distant overseas possessions. Creole elites penetrated the government apparatus as a source of power, prestige, and income. Post-independence *caudillos* habitually used public appointments to reward friends and followers. The multiplication of superfluous government jobs, allocated to poorly qualified candidates on a patronage basis, became a standard means by which twentieth-century populist politicians sought middle-class votes (Bethell 1994b: 9–20, 33–55; Williamson 1992: 374–6).

Latin American constitutional arrangements followed the US model. Presidents chosen through a national vote held executive power, alongside two-chamber legislatures whose members represented local and regional constituencies. The redrawing of constituency boundaries lagged behind the population shift to the cities, so there was a persis-tent over-representation of rural areas, where estate owners remained influential, through customary techniques of patronage and intimida-tion. Also the Catholic church still gave strong support to hierarchical values, especially in the countryside. Often the presidency was held by a populist, elected on a narrow majority or plurality, drawing support mainly from urban workers, and obliged to deal with a legislature in which his conservative opponents had a strong presence. The conflicts and stalemates that resulted were aggravated by the weakness of party structures. Most populist leaders relied above all on charismatic mass appeal. Their parties amounted to little more than personal vehicles, lacking organization or continuity (Bethell 1994b: 108–29).

Furthermore, civilian governments were subject to military interfer-ence. Latin America's armed forces asserted or reasserted a political role in the early 1930s, when they helped to oust export oligarchies weakened by the international economic depression. Since the later nineteenth century, military training had become increasingly rigorous in order to cope with the technical demands of modern warfare, allowing more men from lower- or middle-class backgrounds to gain promotion as officers. They held the traditional landowning elites in low esteem, and favoured industrialization, not least because it would provide a basis for national armaments production (Rouquié 1987: 84–92). But the value which military men placed on discipline made them exasperated at the confusion of civilian politics, and tempted them to intervene as moderators with the aim of restoring stability, by annulling elections or displacing a particular president. So political leaders in office were deterred from risking unpopularity by taking a firm line on contentious issues, while opposition parties were encouraged to be intransigent and obstructive, in the hope of provoking military action from which they might benefit.

Governments could not raise taxes to match the growth of spending on development projects, social welfare, and bureaucracy. It also proved impossible to control inflation, correct exchange rate overvaluation, improve administrative standards, tackle the issue of land reform, or check shanty town settlement. Although politicians used strongly nationalist rhetoric to rally support, maintaining the pace of ISI came to depend on MNC investment. However, when it seemed that budget deficits and inflation were becoming unmanageable, foreign capital inflows ceased. Economic growth came to a halt; political confusion and popular unrest intensified. The military then decided, with considerable civilian approval, that the imminent threat of social breakdown required them to retrieve the situation by taking power into their own hands. The course of events in Brazil between 1950 and 1964, under presidents Vargas, Kubitscheck, Quadros, and Goulart, illustrates this common sequence (Wynia 1990: 219–33).

MILITARY DICTATORSHIPS 1960s–1980s

Military regimes often began by acting more decisively than their civilian predecessors, for example in undertaking land reform (Peru, Ecuador), or in raising extra taxes to correct budget deficits and restore investors' confidence (Brazil, Argentina). Yet sooner or later every country under military rule suffered a recurrence, in aggravated form, of the macroeconomic imbalances that had characterized populist, civilian ISI. The 1980s debt crisis was the result.

First, authoritarian governments made very little progress in eliminating personalism, clientism, and corruption from business and state administration (Evans 1979: 101–62). Failure on this point occurred partly because the attitudes involved were so deeply rooted. Also reform would have to be imposed on upper-class social groups which the military hoped to keep as allies against the radical left. The armed forces did not have a sufficient range of expertise within their own ranks to staff the enterprises and agencies involved in the development effort, establishing a suitably professional, technocratic mentality. For example, the continued influence of economic elites made the Brazilian military regime build its economic strategy round an indiscriminate, wasteful system of subsidies, biased towards large-scale enterprises, and increasingly reliant during the 1970s on foreign borrowing (Frieden 1991:118–25). Business lobbyists obstructed proposals to improve efficiency by exposing national industry to more competition through lower import duties. An excessive emphasis was still given to the production of motor cars and other consumer durables for the middle class.

Military regimes also became susceptible to pressures 'from below'. During the 1960s and 1970s some attempts were made to follow the Cuban model of rural-based insurrection elsewhere in the region, but they succeeded only in Nicaragua. Here the Sandinistas could overthrow the Somoza regime because its narrow, selfish character, effectively rule by a single family, had alienated every level of society, including the urban middle and upper classes. Otherwise, rural rebellions were contained. Governments took note of Batista's downfall, strengthened their security forces, with US backing, and made sure that insurgents did not succeed by default, as had happened on Cuba. Repressive measures were also sufficient to deal with the various clandestine urban guerrilla movements (Bethell 1994b: 198–214, 438–68; Green 1991: 122–31).

The main popular challenges to authoritarianism took other forms, including upsurges of labour unrest. The trade unions built up under state patronage in the populist period were subjected by the military to strict and on the whole effective control. However, a more aggressive 'new unionism' appeared, concentrated among younger workers in the recently established or enlarged automobile and engineering industries. The 1969 *cordobazo*, a wave of strikes and rioting by car workers and university students in the Argentine city of Córdoba, struck a fatal blow against General Onganía's regime (Skidmore and Smith 1997: 99). During the later 1970s the Brazilian military government was weakened by strikes in the motor vehicle factories of the São Paulo region (Cubitt 1995: 187–8; Bethell 1994b: 357–67).

Mass activism extended further with the 'new social movements' (NSMs), neighbourhood associations by which poor people sought to improve their condition through a mixture of self-help and pressure on government for better services. The NSMs provided a means of giving expression to popular discontent when the electoral process was suspended. They were most conspicuous in the shanty towns of the big cities, and received encouragement from the Catholic church, radicalized under the influence of Liberation Theology (Cubitt 1995: 85–7, 194–9; Gilbert 1994: 142–3). Growing agitittation on material issues became linked with demands for a return to democracy. This deterred governments from imposing austerity measures to correct the widening balance of payments deficits caused by the 1970s oil price increases. Reliance was put on foreign borrowing instead (Banuri 1991: 21–4).

The military regimes' basic weakness lay in their lack of sufficient legitimacy. Despite the *caudillo* tradition, and various attempts to establish quasi-fascist ideologies, the assumption prevailed that Latin America's colonial origins and the nineteenth-century independence movements made the region part of a 'Western civilization' in which political pluralism and representative institutions had become the norm. Even the export oligarchies had practised representative government, though with very limited participation. The armed forces claimed that their superior professionalism gave them the right to take charge of national affairs, but only on a temporary basis, as an emergency measure, 'a state of exception'. Bureaucratic authoritarianism intended to restore democracy in a healthier, 'purified' form, an objective which required that account be taken of public opinion, and which complicated the pursuit of development goals (Rouquié 1987: 330–69). In the East Asian NICs, on the other hand, traditions of political mobilization were comparatively weak, and democracy was an alien principle that had not yet put down deep roots, leaving governments with a freer hand to conduct policy on strictly technocratic lines (Haggard 1990: 126–60; Gereffi and Wyman 1990: 139–204).

Chile provides the one notable exception to the Latin American record of weakness and failure under military rule. During the 1950s and 1960s the country had experienced the usual problems of political instability and unviable ISI, culminating in 1970–3 with Salvador Allende's socialist government and its overthrow by a military coup. The initial results of the undiscriminating neoliberal policies followed by General Pinochet's regime after 1973 were unfavourable (Chapter 2), and by 1982 the country laboured under a heavy debt burden. However, since then Chile has made a strong recovery by developing new export lines. The 'non-traditional' export growth owes a good deal to favourable natural resources, but these resources have been reinforced by an unusually high degree of competence and coherence in policy execution. While the basic strategy of raising efficiency through neoliberal measures continued, the errors of the 1973–82 period were recognized, and much more attention was paid to maintaining a stable, competitive REER. Changes in the social welfare system encouraged domestic savings (Chapter 5). Difficult adjustments had to be made at every level of society. Industrialists lost tariff protection. Industrial workers suffered lay-offs and wage cuts. The big landed estates expropriated under Allende were not reconstituted. However, structural reform was pursued long enough to prove its worth. For example, in agriculture medium-sized farms became dominant, their operators imbued with a stronger entrepreneurial spirit, and capable of supplying foreign markets (Hojman 1993; Collins and Lear 1995).

The effectiveness of the Pinochet dictatorship resulted from special circumstances. Chile's public administration has relatively high standards of competence and honesty. Most of the country's population is concentrated within a few hundred miles of the capital city, reducing the need for the patronage techniques associated elsewhere with regionalist tendencies and weak central control. The armed forces enjoy a certain prestige as guardians of the national territory against hostile neighbours, Argentina in particular. Above all, the 1973 coup apparently saved the middle class from socialist revolution, so Pinochet attracted a significant personal following, which enabled him to weather the debt crisis and continue as president until 1989, giving his technocratic advisers a free hand (Frieden 1991:174–7). In Chile the neoliberal approach was apparently justified by results. During the 1990s it has been continued substantially unchanged by elected politicians.

POLITICS SINCE THE DEBT CRISIS

When the Latin American debt crisis began many observers anticipated that economic recession would provoke widespread civil disturbance and an intensification of political conflict, perhaps leading to upheavals of a revolutionary character. So far these expectations have proved unfounded. The military regimes gave up office, peacefully on the whole, and by the early 1990s every country in the region except Cuba had a civilian government based on an election of some kind, even if in many cases the level of authentic democratic participation was questionable (Green 1991: 103–6). Furthermore, all governments, again except Cuba's, were committed with varying degrees of enthusiasm to neoliberal economic reforms. Voters in general have favoured centrist or centre-right presidential candidates. The performance in nationwide elections of left-wing politicians and parties, advocating a socialist or populist approach, has been relatively weak (see Chronology).

The new strength of electoral democracy is due partly to the way that the experience of holding state power left military men, Chile's perhaps excepted, thoroughly chastened by the disappointing results of their stewardship, with no wish to resume responsibility for intractable national problems. The civilian politicians who took over, however unsuccessful in economic management, at least got credit for restoring personal liberties. Traumatic memories remain of the human rights abuses committed under military rule. Few civilians would now consider inviting military intervention, as happened so often in the past. Developments elsewhere gave support to the liberal-democratic cause. Both Spain and Portugal consolidated parliamentary institutions after several decades of dictatorship, challenging the view hitherto current on the Latin American right that democracy was somehow alien to the Iberian heritage (Williamson 1992: 375–7). International communism ceased to represent a plausible threat or provide justification for military coups. The Soviet Union's chronic internal weaknesses became increasingly obvious, leading to its loss of control over Eastern Europe and final breakup in 1989–90. Cold war imperatives no longer inclined the US to back authoritarian regimes.

Electorates have come to support or at least tolerate economic liberalization because of the failure of statist alternatives, as demonstrated by the collapse of Soviet communism, by Latin America's own debt crisis, and by the rampant hyperinflation generated by various 'heterodox' policy experiments attempted in the region during the later 1980s (Chapter 2). In 1994–5 Carlos Menem was re-elected president of Argentina, Alberto Fujimori was re-elected president of Peru, and Fernando Henrique Cardoso was elected president of Brazil, largely on the strength of a commitment to fighting inflation, and with popular mandates to continue neoliberal stabilization measures. Chile's sustained economic recovery since 1984 has apparently shown the value of the neoliberal approach.

Among the poor the loss of faith in activist central government has been expressed through the continued growth of NSM community organizations. Under authoritarian rule many NSMs took a leading role in campaigns for restoring democracy. Once this was achieved they tended to become apolitical, focused on achieving piecemeal improvements through localized cooperative action. Religious trends also suggest a widespread turning away from strategies for taking state power to remedy a harsh material environment. Recently there has been a striking growth of Protestantism within Latin America, eroding the historical ascendancy of the Roman Catholic church, and appealing especially to the underprivileged. The estimated number of Latin American Protestants stood at five million in 1970 and forty million in 1990, their share of the region's population rising from 2 per cent to 10 per cent. As the commitment of most Catholics is relatively weak, they may soon be outnumbered by Protestants among Latin America's regular churchgoers. The general tone of the protestant churches is conservative, emphasizing 'other worldly' spiritual values, combined with personal betterment through self-help and self-discipline. This contrasts with the social-reformist approach of Roman Catholic Liberation Theology, itself a declining force since the 1970s, and may be seen as 'a powerful force of regression back to passivity' (Cubitt 1995: 88). However, diminished popular expectations from government make popular disappointment less likely. Protestants have been conspicuous supporters of politicians advocating neoliberal remedies, for example Alberto Fujimori in Peru (Green 1991: 132–6, 171–84).

CONCLUSION

Latin American society is characterized by unusually marked income differences between rich and poor, a feature that originated in patterns of racial stratification and highly unequal landownership first established during the colonial period. Inequality was perpetuated under twentieth-century ISI by continuing rural poverty, formal/informal-sector occupational divisions in the cities, together with the resilience and adaptability shown by national elites. The various regimes that held power between the 1940s and the 1980s lacked sufficient strength and stability to pursue effective economic programmes. Chile has perhaps recently escaped from the syndrome of social conflict and development failure, but it is still uncertain whether the country can provide a model for the rest of the region. Chile completed the most painful early stages of restructuring under authoritarian military rule. Elsewhere the attempt is now being made to combine democratic politics with neoliberal measures which have further widened income inequality, and so far brought little material benefit to the population at large. Therefore many observers believe that better social welfare provision must play a key role in consolidating democracy and free market reform.

5   Social welfare

So far we have usually taken as our criterion of national development the output of goods and services per head of population, clearly an inadequate guide to welfare standards. Social welfare cannot be measured with any precision, but one commonly used index is infant mortality, the death rate among children less than one year old (Sheahan 1987: 24–7; Abel and Lewis 1993: 33–47). Various other more elaborate 'human development' or 'physical quality of life' indices have been devised, combining infant mortality with literacy, the incidence of gender discrimination, and so forth, but they do not produce substantially different results (Cubitt 1995: 20–3).

Figure 5.1 relates infant mortality and GNP per head for various Latin American and East Asian countries in 1985. (As a comparison, in that year the United Kingdom's GNP per head was US $8,460 and its infant mortality rate stood at 9 per thousand.) Higher levels of output per head are associated with lower infant mortality, but the relationship is not very close. For example, in 1985 China and Bolivia had a similar GNP per head, but China's infant mortality was much lower. Between Chile and Brazil there was an equivalent discrepancy. Judged in this way China and Chile, together with South Korea, may be said to have a relatively good welfare performance, while the record of most Latin American countries is much weaker.

It is also useful to consider changes over time (Figure 5.2). All Latin American countries have experienced a long term fall in infant mortality, but at varying rates, which do not entirely correspond to economic conditions. Thus Chile achieved an unusually rapid infant mortality reduction during the 1970s and early 1980s, when the pace of economic growth was very slow. Over Latin America as a whole infant mortality continued to decline during the later 1980s and early 1990s, despite the economic stresses resulting from the debt crisis. There has also been some recent improvement in education enrolment rates (see p. 75, Table 5.1).

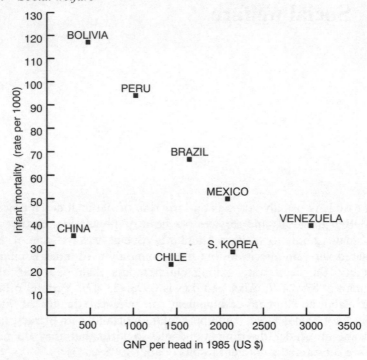

Figure 5.1 Infant mortality* relative to GNP per head, 1985
Note: * Annual deaths per 1,000 among infants aged 0–1 year
Source World Bank 1987: 202–3, 258–9

So while Latin America has made significant gains in social welfare, the standards reached have been rather modest relative to the region's levels of output per head. The shortfall is undesirable in itself and has contributed to economic difficulties. Poor health, nutrition, and education have impaired workers' productive efficiency (Maddison *et al.* 1992: 51–2). On a number of occasions, for example in Brazil during the 1970s, unsatisfactory welfare indicators weakened a government's authority and led to the pursuit of unsustainable spending programmes. The improvement of Latin American social conditions has been limited both by the persistently high levels of income inequality, already discussed in Chapter 4, and by the particular forms that welfare provision have taken, the main concern of this chapter.

WELFARE PROVISION: ORIGINS AND DEVELOPMENT

Latin American welfare services have come to deploy quite substantial resources. On average in the region government social spending

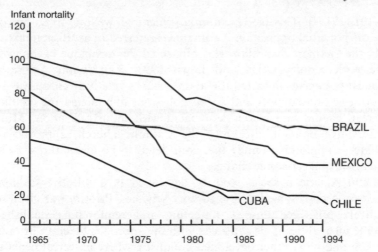

Figure 5.2 Trends in infant mortality, 1965–94
Sources World Bank 1978–96; Díaz-Briquets 1983: 110; Hojman 1993: 58

absorbs about 10 per cent of GNP, less than in the developed countries where the corresponding figure is about 25 per cent, but more than in other parts of the Third World. In the East Asian NICs the share taken is only about 5–7 per cent. Two thirds of East Asian social spending goes to education. Latin America puts more emphasis on health and on social security income maintenance payments (pensions, etc.), categories which overlap and will be discussed together (Maddison *et al.* 1992: 109, 205; World Bank 1991: 66, 225). Education is dealt with separately.

Latin America's distinctive budgetary pattern originated in the early twentieth century when the Southern Cone countries began extending retirement pensions to a wider range of occupational groups. Hitherto such benefits had been confined to a privileged minority of state functionaries: high-ranking military, judges, and other senior officials. Additional pension funds were now established for other groups that showed themselves capable of political or industrial militancy, often including bank clerks, railway and oil industry employees in the first instance, followed by other formal sector urban workers. Coverage reached the urban informal sector and the countryside much more slowly, if at all. As time passed, other countries embarked on the same course, Brazil in the 1930s, Mexico in the 1940s. Retirement pensions were supplemented by health insurance, maternity allowances, unemployment, sickness, invalidity and child benefits (Maddison *et al.* 1992:

96–101, 191–3). This piecemeal enlargement of welfare, to co-opt or buy off potential opposition is sometimes referred to as 'Bismarckian', after the German chancellor who pioneered the technique in the later nineteenth century (Abel and Lewis 1993: 3–6). Latin American populist politicians favoured the approach as a relatively cheap way to secure electoral support and social cohesion, minimizing the conflict between capital and labour associated with industrialization. More conservative opinion, including the Catholic church, approved of welfare as reinforcing family life, considered to be under threat from secularism and economic change.

Latin American social security developed in a selective fashion, based on occupation-specific insurance schemes. Priority was given to relatively privileged groups, reflecting and reinforcing established income inequalities. This contrasts with the approach taken in Britain, the US, and most other developed countries, where universal benefits were financed from general government revenues, including progressive income tax paid at higher rates by the rich, redistributing purchasing power to the poor. In continental Europe, where practice originally evolved along 'Bismarckian' lines, welfare provision became effectively universal and redistributive by the mid-twentieth century.

Latin American welfare systems have had many weaknesses. First, provision has been highly discriminatory and stratified, with the most generous benefits received by the more affluent, and the least help going to those with the greatest need. In the 1970s about 40 per cent of the region's population still lacked any insurance cover, and remained dependent on residual public health services (Abel and Lewis 1993: 49–74). For example, the Mexican government's health spending per head for state employees, beneficiaries of the ISSTE insurance fund, was nearly twice that for private-sector employees under the inferior IMSS scheme, and twenty times greater than for the uninsured population (Maddison *et al.* 1992: 202). There was a marked urban bias in the distribution of services. Within the cities, hospitals and clinics were disproportionately concentrated at central locations, so that poorer people living in irregular suburban settlements commonly resorted to private treatment at their own expense, even when they had insurance, because of the long journeys required to attend state facilities (Ward 1990: 155–67).

Apart from the inequality of provision, the methods used to finance Latin American social security have also had many undesirable features. Schemes were usually funded in the first instance partly by employees' contributions and partly by payroll charges on employers. Employees' contributions could often be set against income tax liability, a feature that was most useful to the higher paid. Payroll levies gained favour in Latin America partly because they were relatively easy to collect, an important consideration for countries with weakly developed administrative structures. Also charges which fell on capitalist enterprises, many of them foreign-owned, were more politically acceptable than taxes paid by the wider public.

By the 1970s social security contributions were typically adding 50 per cent to the wage bill of large-scale Latin American businesses, impairing export competitiveness, encouraging the use of labour-saving technology, and limiting the growth of formal-sector employment. For example, cane-cutting machines had been adopted on Peru's coastal sugar estates as a response to the unionization of the labour force and the introduction of social security arrangements (Abel and Lewis 1993: 160–1). Under ISI many large firms with a monopoly or near-monopoly position in their protected national markets could pass on extra payroll costs by charging higher prices. This outcome was likely to be regressive, bearing heavily on poorer consumers with little or no welfare coverage who financed benefits received by the more affluent.

Usually pension and other social security schemes were first set up on a 'funded' basis. It was intended that participants' contributions should be invested in productive assets, generating an income stream from which future obligations could be met. ECLA economists justified welfare provision as a means of generating capital for development projects. But as time passed surpluses were eroded by the growing number of claimants, and by the granting of excessively generous benefits, in response to political pressures. Many employees in higher-grade occupations became entitled to retire on full pay in their forties or fifties, after as little as twenty years' service. They could then take up another well-paid job, perhaps leading to another pension. The most privileged workers, those who could retire earliest, tended to have the longest life expectancy and so put the heaviest burden on pension funds. Social security institutions rarely succeeded in building up an investment stock to match the multiplying demands placed upon them. Pension contributions were used to subsidize medical services. Reserves suffered depletion through being lent to governments at low rates of interest that did not keep pace with inflation. In Argentina social security income covered mounting losses on the railways, most of them formerly British-owned, after they were brought under state control by Perón during the late 1940s. The network was used to create jobs for Perón's trade union supporters, and soon became grossly overmanned (Abel and Lewis 1993: 187–95).

Thus instead of being funded, an instrument for raising national savings rates, Latin American social security became 'pay as you go', with current income used to meet current outgoings. Many schemes went into deficit as contributions lagged behind the growth of entitlements. Governments then felt obliged to meet shortfalls by inflationary finance (printing money), and by general taxation that fell most heavily on the poor. To the extent that welfare provision offered, or seemed to offer, a guaranteed income, people may have been discouraged from building up their own savings for emergencies and old age. In East Asia the comparative weakness of democratic pressures allowed governments to keep social security outlays at minimal levels. Some neoliberals argue that this has been an important cause of the region's unusually high rates of personal or household savings, and its limited reliance on foreign capital.

Finally, the profusion of occupation-specific schemes raised administrative costs. For example, thirty-five different social security funds were established in Chile; Cuba before the 1959 revolution had more than fifty. Individual funds developed their own hospital networks, distinct from, and greatly superior to the services maintained by national ministries of health for those without insurance. So there was much duplicated investment, and a low occupancy rate in many of the best facilities, from which the uninsured population was excluded. The channelling of resources towards occupational schemes encouraged an emphasis on curative medicine and the neglect of preventive public health measures, such as mass screening or immunization campaigns. Nomination to appointments in welfare bureaucracies served as a widely used form of political patronage. Administrations became noted for their opulent head office buildings and generous salary scales. In Latin America management costs absorbed about 10 per cent of social security expenditure, compared with the norm of 3 per cent or less found in developed countries.

Some of the authoritarian military governments that took power during the 1960s and 1970s tried to put social security on a more coherent basis. Brazil's post-1964 regime unified provision for private-sector workers, eliminating the separate occupational funds with their trade union representation on management boards. Coverage was extended to a much larger share of the labour force, including rural workers. The aims were to cut administrative costs, legitimize military rule, and end the use of social security schemes as a trade union power base. Bringing in extra contributors would raise the national savings rate. In practice, however, benefit levels remained grossly unequal, while the reliance on regressive payroll taxes and the shift towards curative treatment at the expense of public health measures continued. Public hospitals were unable to meet the growth of demand, and the contracting out of services to private clinics resulted in large-scale overcharging and fraud, for the benefit of a powerful 'medico-pharmaceutical complex'. When party politics resumed under the *abertura* of the later 1970s, clientage and patronage superseded technocractic rationality in appointments to the social security bureaucracy. The economic crisis of the 1980s plunged the whole system into deficit (Abel and Lewis 1993: 341–64; Maddison *et al.* 1992: 96–101).

On Cuba the post-1959 revolutionary government pursued a vigorous programme for improving welfare by redistributive measures on behalf of the poor, by replacing stratified occupational funds with a comprehensive benefit system, and extending health services into rural areas. The effects of these changes in reducing malnutrition and infant mortality have attracted admiring comment (Cubitt 1995: 95–6). However, at the time of the revolution conditions here were already quite favourable. An abundance of good quality farmland suitable for sugar growing, combined with ready access to North American markets, capital, and technology, had given Cuba one of Latin America's highest levels of income per head, and a relatively low infant mortality rate. Unequal property ownership and chronic unemployment outside the months of the sugar cane harvest limited the benefits reaching agricultural workers, but popular living standards were still well above the regional norm. After 1959 the US trade embargo, mismanaged attempts at economic diversification, and the loss of labour discipline associated with the transition from capitalism to socialism, all took their toll. In the late 1970s the island's output per head was no higher than it had been twenty years before (Sheahan 1987: 45–7, 246). (For Latin America as a whole output per head rose 70 per cent over the same period.) A third of Cuba's doctors left the country during the first three years following the revolution, as part of a larger middle-class exodus. These circumstances held back welfare gains. A detailed demographic study suggests that only about a quarter of the eleven-year increase in life expectancy at birth which occurred in Cuba between 1953 and 1970 is attributable to the revolution (Díaz-Briquets 1983: 120–5).

WELFARE SINCE THE DEBT CRISIS

It might be expected that the debt crisis and the subsequent shift towards neoliberal economic policies must have had very damaging consequences for Latin American welfare. During the 1980s an average decline of about 5 per cent in regional income per head was accompanied by widening inequality. The rich suffered little, if at all. Revenues from their holdings of flight capital were payable in foreign currency, and therefore not curtailed by exchange devaluations. Since 1982 creditors have usually enjoyed high real interest rates. On the other hand, urban formal sector real wages commonly fell by 20 or 30 per cent. Price levels were pushed up by devaluations and by the elimination of consumer subsidies to cut fiscal deficits. Unemployment rose. Social programmes were curtailed as foreign debt service payments took a growing share of government budgets (Abel and Lewis 1993: 75–107; Bulmer-Thomas 1994: 400–3). Thus in Mexico between 1977 and 1986 public spending on social services as a share of GNP declined from 4.7 per cent to 2.4 per cent; for Bolivia the corresponding figures are 3.5 per cent and 1.7 per cent (Bethell 1994b: 82).

Some authors therefore argue that a severe deterioration in general well-being occurred:

> The poor majority were made to bear the brunt of the debt crisis through hunger and increased poverty, while those who had squandered the loans or spirited them abroad remained untouched . . . . Advances in health and nutrition went into reverse; more Latin American children were malnourished or dying in the 1980s than ten years previously.
>
> (Green 1991: 76–7)

'Health, nutrition, infant mortality, educational enrolment and food consumption have all suffered' (Abel and Lewis 1993: 96). In fact, matters are not so clear-cut. Most Latin Americans certainly suffered declining income per head during the 1980s, but at the same time improvements in infant mortality and other social indicators continued. The reasons for these discrepancies are not yet firmly established, so here we can only mention various factors that may have mitigated the recession's welfare effects.

Austerity, liberalization, and structural adjustment programmes have fallen most heavily on employees in government and ISI industries. These urban formal sector workers had previously received incomes quite considerably above the subsistence margin, and so could maintain nutritional standards, despite falling wages, by curtailing non-food expenditures. There is some evidence for dietary deterioration immediately after the onset of the debt crisis, but by 1990 food supplies per head in most countries matched the levels current ten years earlier (Goodman and Redclift 1991: 65–7; FAO 1995: 233–6). Most of the poorest Latin Americans are still in agriculture, which has been comparatively resilient, especially where opportunities remain for frontier colonization, and where illicit drugs production is flourishing (Chapters 3 and 7; Bethell 1994a: 386–7). International migration, mainly to the US, has been an important means of relief from adversity in Mexico and the Caribbean basin.

Within Latin American cities the undoubted decline of formal-sector employment and wage rates was offset to some extent by the compensatory growth of the unrecorded informal economy. More married women have taken up street trading and similar activities, to supplement household budgets. The spread of contraception and falling birth rates have helped women's entry to the paid labour force (Chapter 6). The fertility decline has improved infants' survival chances, which have also benefited from the development of cheaper vaccines and new medical techniques, such as the oral rehydration therapy used for cases of dysentery and diarrhoea.

It is possible that health standards continued to rise, despite the recession and curtailed public spending, on the basis of investments made before the debt crisis in facilities, equipment, and the training of medical personnel. During the 1960s and 1970s the number of qualified Latin American doctors and nurses was considerably enlarged. Even when the real salary level of health workers was cut as an economy measure after 1982 their expertise was still usually available (Maddison *et al.* 1992: 201–2). Nevertheless, on the whole it seems unlikely that improvements occurring primarily as a lagged response to earlier outlays would have been sustained for so long.

The rise in housing costs for the urban poor has probably been rather modest. Government programmes of subsidized house building have been cut, but they had never brought much benefit to the lowest income groups. Homeowners were able to economize by delaying repairs and improvements. Tenancies commonly ran for several years, so landlords could not raise rents to keep up with more rapid rates of increase in the general price level. The ending of large construction projects made skilled labour more readily available for self-help housing. Most building materials are national products rather than imports, limiting the cost effects of devaluation (Abel and Lewis 1993: 120–6).

Some efforts have been made to limit the human costs of adjustment by directing social expenditures in a more precise, selective fashion. For example, until the early 1980s the Mexican government maintained general food subsidies, much of the benefits from which went to relatively affluent consumers, while low-income peasant farmers were obliged to sell their crops at controlled prices. The cost of government subsidies on basic products had reached 10 per cent of

GNP (Abel and Lewis 1993: 120). After 1982 these arrangements were replaced by a more economical system of subsidized food rations targeted at poor families. Other examples of selective spending include the Emergency Social Fund set up in 1986 by the Bolivian government to alleviate the distress resulting from austerity measures, and Mexico's Solidarity Programme (Maddison *et al.* 1992: 203–4; Gilbert 1994: 151–3). These schemes bypassed established bureaucracies and enlisted local community cooperation, with the aim of minimizing implementation costs and maximizing benefits to the poor.

The fashion for targeting and selectivity in provision has been combined with measures decentralizing welfare administration, handing over responsibilities to local- and private-sector agencies. This trend draws support from a broad range of opinion, including both neoliberals and their post-modernist critics, reflecting the widespread agreement reached that central government, at least under Latin American conditions, has a natural tendency to become bureaucratic, patronage-ridden, and corrupt. Localized bodies, it is hoped, will be more accountable to the public and therefore more effective.

Chile under the Pinochet dictatorship provides the most notable example of a neoliberal assault on centralized public welfare. Resources were shifted away from hospitals in the major cities to more widely dispersed primary health care clinics under local municipal control, committed to the delivery of preventive measures such as immunization and education in basic hygiene. Targeted programmes distributed food to pregnant women and young children (Gilbert 1994: 151; World Bank 1990: 85). Major cost savings were made, because less was spent on elaborate equipment, and because pay rates for medical staff were lower in the municipal sector than in the unionized central government service. The Pinochet regime could override hitherto powerful professional vested interests and pressure groups, but the changes made did ensure that the decline of infant mortality continued, despite cuts in health spending per head, and deteriorating economic conditions (Figure 5.2). Critics of Chile's neoliberal policies argue that the undoubted progress on infant mortality was achieved by neglecting other health issues, resulting for example in epidemics of typhoid fever and hepatitis (Collins and Lear 1995: 117–23). However, the reduction of infant mortality has been accompanied by a fall in the death rate for the population as a whole at a more rapid pace than in most other Latin American countries (World Bank 1993: 290–3).

The Chilean reforms were politically autocratic in tone. Decentralized provision elsewhere has put more emphasis on popular participation through local community action, of the type made conspicuous by the new social movements (NSMs) that proliferated in Latin America from the 1970s (Chapter 4). NSMs demanded better government services, but there was often also a strong commitment to self-help. For example, shanty town neighbours might work together on building a health clinic, extending a school, paving streets, or laying water pipes, perhaps using materials provided by state agencies. Such initiatives have received a good deal of support from NGOs (non-governmental organizations) or PVOs (private voluntary organizations, the equivalent US expression), terms now commonly applied to a wide range of non-official bodies. While most NGOs operate on a small-scale, local basis, some are national or international in scope. As well as the thousands which have appeared in Latin America and other developing regions, there are large numbers based in the developed countries which are concerned with the Third World; for example Oxfam, Care, and Save the Children.

NGOs rely on voluntary support, but also employ paid, full-time specialists (lawyers, doctors, engineers, architects, etc.). During Latin America's period of military rule professionals and academics excluded for political reasons from government or university posts often found work in the NGO sector. The Roman Catholic church's engagement with social issues under the influence of Liberation Theology (Chapter 4) provided another important source of leadership. Because of their flexibility, moral commitment, and demonstrated capacity for liaising with poor people through small-scale projects, NGOs now attract a good deal of international development aid, and often serve as vehicles for targeted social spending by Latin American governments.

Community-based initiatives have many weaknesses. Only a small minority of the poor, rarely more than 10 per cent in urban areas, involve themselves with neighbourhood associations. Participation is limited by the daily struggle to make a living and care for children. Economic and occupational differences between households restrict any sense of collective identity (Gilbert 1994: 130–1). The economic crisis of the 1980s, it is suggested, has increased residential mobility and community fragmentation, leaving individual or family action as the main element in survival strategies (Bethell 1994a: 311–12). The NGOs' effectiveness has been impaired by the hostility of state bureaucracies, poor coordination, political factionalism, and attempts to impose middle-class ideological preoccupations on poorer clients (Abel and Lewis 1993: 421–37). On the other hand, the growth of NSMs under authoritarian rule and during the return to democracy often does seem to have raised neighbourhood consciousness and confidence, not least by involving significant numbers of women in public life for the first time (Chapter 6). NGOs, with their accumulating experience and networks of professional or semi-professional activists, have become a significant social force in several countries. So it may be that grassroots mobilizations have helped to limit the effect of the debt crisis on Latin American welfare, both by their own self-help activities (communal kitchens and cooperative building work, for example), and by ensuring that in a period of severe budgetary constraint, governments take fuller account of popular needs.

Pension provision is another aspect of social policy that has attracted considerable attention. As noticed earlier, state pension systems were originally established on a funded basis, partly with a view to generating capital for development, but over time populist pressures made them 'pay as you go' and often insolvent. Chile's military dictatorship pioneered pensions reform in the late 1970s by introducing a new system of privately managed funds (*AFP*s) to replace the established state schemes. The restructuring eliminated employers' payments, seen as a burden on business enterprise. Participating employees' future pension rights were related more strictly to contributions made, with the aim of avoiding deficits and generating surpluses. It was hoped that competition between funds to attract participants by offering the most favourable returns would improve administrative efficiency. Also fund managers would pay closer attention to the quality of investments made, ensuring that assets were used productively and not depleted through wasteful state spending, as had happened so often in the past (Collins and Lear 1995: 167–81). Critics of neoliberalism question the efficiency of Chile's privatized schemes, arguing that the *AFP*s' aggressive advertising and sales campaigns have made management charges more burdensome than under the previous arrangements (Collins and Lear 1995: 176). Nevertheless, since the early 1980s Chile's savings rate has risen quite considerably, reducing dependence on foreign capital. So the Chilean approach to pension reform has attracted a number of imitators, though whether it can succeed elsewhere remains doubtful (Chapter 8).

EDUCATION

Latin America's public education systems have grown substantially during the twentieth century and, in principle at least, expansion occurred on an egalitarian, universalist basis, contrasting with the stratified approach taken for health and social security services. Education was seen as an instrument to secure national unity, integrating immigrant and indigenous Indian populations. This required comprehensive coverage under central control. By the 1940s most Latin American countries had made school attendance compulsory and free for young children. By 1960 high levels of primary school enrolment had been reached (Table 5.1) and about two thirds of the adult population was reported as literate. Educational trends in the East Asian NICs up to that date appear broadly similar.

However, Latin American education showed serious qualitative defects, with frequent pupil absences, dropping out, and grade repetition, especially at the primary level. These weaknesses persist. In recent years less than half those entering Colombia's primary schools complete the four-year curriculum (Abel and Lewis 1993: 138). About three quarters of Brazil's adults declared themselves literate in the 1980 census, although at that date only 41 per cent of the country's adult population had completed the four years of basic education considered necessary to acquire functional literacy (Maddison *et al.* 1992: 87). Such problems result partly from variations between schools in expenditure levels. Much of the revenue for educational services is raised locally, to the detriment of standards in rural areas with a limited tax base. Ethnic, linguistic, and class differences impair teachers' communication with their pupils. In the East Asian NICs, on the other hand, education benefits from the greater degree of cultural uniformity. Higher population densities make it easier to enforce compulsory attendance laws, and ensure that young children have access to schools of a viable size. So good quality primary schooling was established here by the 1950s, providing a much better basis than in Latin America for the subsequent growth of secondary education. Latin America then suffered during the 1960s and 1970s from a disproportionate, lavishly funded expansion of university education, undertaken in response to pressure from the higher income groups,

Table 5.1 Proportions of age groups enrolled in education, 1960–92 (%)

	Primary education*			Secondary education			Higher education		
	1960	1980	1992	1960	1980	1992	1960	1979	1992
Brazil	95	93	106	11	32	39	2	12	12
Mexico	80	120	113	11	37	55	3	15	14
Chile	109	117	96	24	55	72	4	12	23
South Korea	94	107	105	27	85	90	5	14	42

Note: * Enrolment rates in excess of 100 per cent occur when older children attend primary school
Sources World Bank 1983: 197; World Bank 1995: 217

and mainly for their benefit. The university sector came to take about 40 per cent of state education spending in the region (compared with 10–20 per cent in East Asia), at the expense of primary and secondary schools (ECLAC 1992: 37–61).

There are conflicting views about the impact of the debt crisis on Latin American education. Some authors argue that economic recession made more children drop out of school so that they could work and contribute to hard-pressed family budgets (Gilbert 1994: 77). However, official statistics show a continued rise in enrolment rates, concentrated at the secondary level (Table 5.1). It is suggested that the trend may be partly 'inertial'. Previous educational expansion has raised the proportion of parents who have had some schooling themselves, and who therefore want their own children to remain at school. Also recession reduced the employment available for children, and the opportunity cost of keeping them out of the labour market (ECLAC 1992: 41). Intensified competition for job opportunities increased the importance attached to educational qualifications (Roberts 1995: 130).

For education, as for health and social security, Chile offers the most controversial example of neoliberal reform. The Pinochet regime cut back the university sector's share of a severely reduced educational budget, and gave elementary schooling a higher priority. Public universities were obliged to cover most of their costs from tuition fees. Private institutions, operating on a commercial basis, were allowed greater freedom to compete for students and state subsidies. The aim was to raise efficiency and encourage more vocationally oriented teaching. The changes have been followed by what is in Latin American terms a relatively strong growth of enrolment rates at both secondary and higher levels (Table 5.1), but there are doubts about the standards of provision. Some studies claim that, despite cuts in public spending, the government maintained quality by ensuring an adequate supply of educational materials (World Bank 1990: 117). Others dispute this (Abel and Lewis 1993: 439–51; Collins and Lear 1995: 125–48). Also, political circumstances would make it very difficult to follow a similar course elsewhere. For example, while Argentina's 1976–83 military rulers limited enrolment in the country's public university system, their civilian successors felt obliged to affirm their democratic commitment by restoring an open admissions policy with free tuition.

CONCLUSION

Latin American welfare standards have risen over the last half century, but progress has been limited by the bias of state services towards the relatively affluent. Occupationally stratified insurance schemes for better paid formal-sector workers have taken a large share of spending, at the expense of public health measures and primary education. Although the 1980s debt crisis brought sharp reductions in real income for much of the population, infant mortality, an important welfare indicator, has continued to decline. This trend apparently results from better medical techniques and the more effective targeting of social outlays, perhaps reinforced by stronger self-help activism among the poor. Social welfare improvements may therefore have helped to support democratic 'centrist' politics under difficult circumstances. However, Latin American educational standards still give serious cause for concern, and without major reform in this area a strong economic recovery is unlikely. The post-modernist left probably exaggerates the benefits likely to come from grassroots initiatives. Chile's military dictatorship made considerable welfare gains, while severely discouraging popular mobilization. Elsewhere, NGO-promoted schemes for shanty town upgrading leave in place a fundamentally inefficient pattern of urban settlement.

6 Women

In Latin America, as everywhere else, women's status is inferior to that of men. Many accounts note how gender relations in the region have been shaped by the notion of *machismo*, an attitude among men that puts an exaggerated emphasis on masculine power and virility. The mentality is believed to have originated from medieval Iberian traditions of chivalry and militarism, reinforced by the process of transatlantic colonial conquest. Support for this interpretation comes from the fact that within Latin America *macho* values are least pronounced among those indigenous populations that have kept the greatest measure of autonomy from external influences. *Machismo* sanctions male aggression and assertiveness, the 'double standard' of sexual behaviour (chastity and fidelity required of women but not men), and female exclusion from the public sphere. At the same time *marianismo*, an ethos of female spirituality, resignation, humility, and fortitude, derived from the Roman Catholic church's cult of the Virgin Mary, is said to have allowed Latin American women some influence at home (Skidmore and Smith 1997: 62–3; Green 1991: 139–40). However, it is doubtful whether Latin American views on gender have differed much from the patriarchal, chauvinistic male attitudes long familiar in the developed countries. *Machismo/marianismo* never entailed the rigorous female seclusion and subjection found in much of South Asia and the Islamic Middle East. Women's life expectancy and educational attainments compare more favourably with those of men in Latin America than in other Third World regions (Table 6.1). We must also take note of Latin American women's increased participation in the labour force, their declining fertility, and the changes in their political role that have occurred during the course of the twentieth century.

Table 6.1 Male/female differentials in life expectancy and education, 1965–93

	Female life expectancy at birth as a % of male			Females in education per 100 males					
				Primary			Secondary		
	1965	1988	1993	1965	1987	1992	1965	1987	1992
Latin America	107	109	109	95	96	95	77	110	104
East Asia	106	99	106	n.a.	84	89	50	71	78
South Asia	98	100	100	54	n.a.	73	34	n.a.	56
Sub-Saharan Africa	105	106	106	56	77	81	36	59	72
Middle East	n.a.	n.a.	103	70	n.a.	83	88	n.a.	79
Developed countries	110	108	108	95	95	95	93	100	98

Sources World Bank 1990: 241; World Bank 1991: 267; World Bank 1995: 219

WOMEN IN THE LABOUR FORCE

By international standards Latin American women's labour force participation has been rather low (Table 6.2), originally because of their limited employment in agriculture. The plough cultivation and cattle ranching characteristic of the region involves tasks considered too arduous for women. Also, estate operations are often performed by gang labour. Men have been reluctant to allow their female dependants to do such work, alongside or under the authority of males from outside the household circle. In Latin America there has been less scope for employing women on peasant family farms than, for example in East Asia, where smallholder rice cultivation entails much transplanting and weeding labour. Estate mechanization has cut back further the role of women in Latin American agriculture, a trend offset to only a limited degree by their use in some new export lines, such as Colombia's cut flower production, and Chile's fruit growing (Bethell 1994b, 484–8).

The growth of Latin American female employment over recent decades resulting from economic development and urbanization has been concentrated in service occupations. The expansion of the middle classes enlarged the demand for domestic maidservants. Women became prominent in the urban informal sector, as street vendors and laundresses for example. Females have also gained ground in the formal sector, as secretaries or other subordinate clerical employees in government, commerce, and finance, as shop assistants, as teachers (mainly at the primary level), and in medicine (mainly as nurses). Women's growing access to university education has allowed them to gain higher professional status, for example as doctors and lawyers, in

Table 6.2 Women as a proportion of the labour force, 1960 and 1993 (%)[*]

	1960	1993
Latin America	19	27
East Asia	37	42
South Asia	28	22
Sub-Saharan Africa	36	37
Middle East	8	16
Developed countries	32	38

Note: * These figures do not include the unpaid domestic work undertaken by women
for their own families
Sources World Bank 1984c: 149, 158–9; World Bank 1995: 219

small but significant numbers. Women now account for about half of
Latin America's service employment.

However, women's role in manufacturing industry has been quite
modest. They provided roughly 20 per cent of the region's industrial
labour force in 1960, and 25 per cent by 1990. The corresponding
figures for the East Asian NICs are 20 per cent in 1960, and 45 per
cent in 1990. Part of the difference may result from the emphasis of
Latin American ISI manufacturing on 'heavy' industry (steelmaking,
engineering, etc.), and the weakness of 'light' export-oriented assembly
work (clothing, electronics), where in East Asia females commonly
take 80–90 per cent of the jobs. But even when comparison is made on
an industry by industry basis, Latin American women's share of
employment is still relatively low. In addition, certain industries have
experienced a marked decline of women's employment share over time,
for example in textile factories from about 70 per cent during the early
decades of the twentieth century to about 30 per cent by the 1970s.

Some authors attribute the displacement of female labour to investment in more advanced and highly automated machinery (Cubitt 1995:
117), but technical change has not had this result in East Asia.
Therefore it is more likely that the recruitment of women into Latin
American manufacturing has been limited by the protective legislation
on their behalf introduced during the first half of the twentieth
century. Such provisions raised the cost to employers of female labour
and discouraged its use. The measures included the prohibition of
women from hazardous occupations, controls on women's working
hours (especially the outlawing of night work by women), entitlements
to paid maternity leave, the establishment of nurseries for children,
and equality of pay with men doing the same tasks. These regulations
were sought by unionized male workers, influenced by European
socialist thought, as a defence against competition in the labour

market from 'exploited' women. Populist politicians were highly sympathetic to female employment protection, an issue on which they could enlist general support. Even landowning elites welcomed regulation, as a restraint on the development of capitalist industry (Bethell 1994b: 488–99).

When the authoritarian governments of the 1960s and 1970s sought to promote capitalist development by curbing trade union rights, few attempts were made at reducing legal controls on the employment of women. The military regimes' social conservatism included the belief that 'a woman's place is at home'; they had no wish to make the mobilization of female labour an important part of their economic strategy. The 1980s brought a return to democracy and some growth in women's political influence, or at least in government expressions of concern for their interests (see below). Under these circumstances little has been done to weaken female employment protection, despite the general fashion for economic liberalization.

It is true that the enforcement of Latin American employment laws has usually been lax, so they have only had a substantial effect on employment practice in larger, formal-sector establishments. Common techniques for evasion include the dispersal of tasks among unregulated informal-sector subcontractors, or the use of women as outworkers in their own homes, sewing up garments for example. Factory workers can be frequently replaced, so that they do not qualify for the benefits available to longer-term employees. However, with subcontracting and outworking it is difficult to achieve internationally acceptable levels of standardization and quality. Economies of scale are lost. High employee turnover as a means of limiting entitlement to regulatory coverage obstructs the accumulation of workforce experience and skills.

As a contrast, East Asian factories have been less affected by workplace regulation, allowing them to recruit and employ larger proportions of women, a useful competitive advantage. In East Asia, as elsewhere, the strength of patriarchal assumptions has made women, by comparison with men, more flexible and tractable as workers, tolerant of lower wage rates, and more profitable to employ for those manufacturing occupations that do not require great physical strength or long training. Institutional restraints on the employment of women have constituted one more disadvantage for Latin American industry, adding to its many other problems (Chapter 2). The disadvantage seems likely to continue. The assembly plants set up in the *maquiladora* belt along the US–Mexican border and in the Caribbean basin export processing zones have a greater proportion of women workers than does Latin American industry as a whole, but their labour forces are less thoroughly feminized than those of similar East Asian factories. Moreover, export assembly remains a very small element in Latin American manufacturing. Thus the growth of female employment within the region during the 1980s resulted mainly from women taking up unregulated informal-sector service work, as they tried to maintain household income in the face of economic recession and the consequent decline of male earnings (Chant 1991; Roberts 1995: 128–30).

After 1959 Cuba's revolutionary government encouraged women to work outside the home, as a form of self-liberation and public service, by providing nursery schools, crèches, and public laundries. Such measures had only a limited effect. Apart from the lower proportion of domestic servants, female employment patterns on the island do not differ much from those found elsewhere in Latin America (Bethell 1994b: 493–4; Cubitt 1995: 119–21). One factor limiting Cuban women's entry to the labour market has been the need for them to spend much of their time standing in queues to obtain rationed commodities, another feature of life under socialism (Sheahan 1987: 248).

CONTRACEPTION AND THE BIRTH RATE

Latin American birth rates have fallen over the last 30 years, broadly matching trends elsewhere (Table 6.3), and to a considerable degree representing no more than the local expression of world-wide 'modernization' processes. In the past it could often be useful to have many children, as extra labour on peasant farms, as an insurance against high infant mortality, and as a support for parents in their old age. These benefits from large families have been reduced or eliminated by economic development, urbanization, medical advances, and state social provision. Infants' survival chances have improved. Increased education has raised women's aspirations and the cost of bringing up children. New consumer durables have become available, competing for a larger share of household budgets and making the costs of child maintenance seem more burdensome. All these influences have been at work in Latin America, rather less powerfully than in the developed countries, but more so than in Africa, for example, where economic progress has been minimal.

Nevertheless, the pace of Latin America's fertility decline cannot be entirely explained in these terms, because during the 1960s and 1970s the birth rate was brought down more sharply in the East Asian NICs, before they had caught up with Latin American levels of income per

Table 6.3 Crude birth rates, 1965 and 1993 (births per 1,000 population)

	1965	1993
Latin America	40	26
East Asia	39	21
South Asia	45	31
Sub-Saharan Africa	48	44
Middle East	48	33
Developed countries	20	13

Sources World Bank 1989: 217; World Bank 1995: 213

head, urbanization, and industrialisation. An important source of difference, it seems, was national attitudes and culture; there was less inclination to accept population control in Latin America than in East Asia. In Latin American countries the Catholic church and its teaching against contraception had a considerable influence, at least among the ruling circles which determined official policy. Certainly it was out of the question for Latin American governments (except in revolutionary Cuba) to make abortion facilities as freely available as in East Asia. Furthermore, Latin American policy makers were suspicious of birth control as an 'imperialist' panacea, apparently recommended by richer countries because it offered a low-cost alternative to development aid. There was much distaste for the aggressive measures to limit population growth implemented during the 1950s by the US in Puerto Rico, its Caribbean dependency. The programme included the widespread use of the contraceptive pill, at that time a recent and untested invention.

Larger populations were widely believed to be necessary for ensuring the development of abundant natural resources, providing an adequate domestic market for ISI, and increasing national military strength. (The armed forces claimed demographic policy as their special concern.) So while the small East Asian NICs, more obviously threatened by overpopulation, became vigorously committed to birth control from the early 1960s, Latin American governments were not persuaded of the need to restrain population growth until the later 1970s, when economic prospects were clouded by growing foreign indebtedness (World Bank 1984: 170–2, 200–1; Wynia 1990: 129–31). Since then official policy has become more tolerant of contraception, without doing much to actively encourage it. A number of large-scale private programmes have been established to promote family planning; sterilization is the most widely used method. Another recent change which has probably contributed to the Latin American birth rate decline is the growth of women's political activism and their increased self-confidence in relations with male partners (see below). Also, the economic recession and the extra pressure on women to seek paid work has encouraged them to limit their fertility (Radcliffe and Westwood 1993: 192; Bethell 1994a: 17–27, 48–56; Green 1991: 142–3).

WOMEN AND POLITICS

During the middle decades of the twentieth century women gained voting rights throughout Latin America, with Ecuador the first country where female suffrage was granted, in 1929, and Paraguay the last, in 1961. The concession was made following the European and North American examples, as part of the wider democratic challenge to the traditional oligarchic order. The same influences also prompted efforts to improve female education, taken as a sign of modernity and progress. Educated women, it was thought, would contribute to national development by being better mothers, who brought up their children as informed, useful citizens. By the 1970s women's illiteracy rates had been cut to about 30 per cent, compared with about 25 per cent among men, the widest differences remaining in the poorest countries (Bethell 1994b: 520–8; Cubitt 1995: 113).

Initially at least, however, these developments did not give women any significant weight in the political process. Very few secured electoral office. Their voting behaviour usually seems to have closely followed that of men. The small minority of women who entered government were mainly confined to policy areas stereotyped as 'feminine': social welfare, education, health, and culture. In the populist period the only woman who took a notable public role was Juan Perón's wife Eva (Evita). During his first term as president of Argentina (1946–51) she established a remarkable mass appeal through personal charisma and her work in dispensing social benefits. Overwhelming support from newly enfranchised women voters enabled Juan Perón to secure re-election under difficult circumstances in 1951. But Evita died the following year. She had always subscribed to conventional principles of female subordination, and her legacy did not prevent Perón's overthrow by a military coup in 1955. Women's role in Peronism dwindled, and the movement's subsequent strength derived above all from its predominantly male trade union base (Skidmore and Smith 1997: 88–91).

Rather paradoxically, women became more prominent in Latin American public life under the military dictatorships of the 1970s. Mobilization took three main forms: human rights campaigns, feminist groups (these first two largely middle class), and neighbourhood associations involving poorer women over economic or welfare demands.

The best-known women's human rights movement was begun in Argentina in 1977 by mothers seeking information about their children who had disappeared through the military regime's indiscriminate 'dirty war' against radical subversion and terrorism. The repression, which claimed at least 10,000 victims of kidnapping, torture and secret execution, fell with greatest severity on young people. The mothers of the disappeared began holding weekly protest meetings at the Plaza de Mayo in Buenos Aires, where they attracted international publicity. The regime, committed to a traditionalist rhetoric extolling 'family values' and the role of motherhood, felt unable to act with its usual harshness against the demonstrators. The mothers of the Plaza de Mayo kept alive the question of human rights abuses and made an important contribution to the wave of popular protests that forced the military junta from office in 1983 after the Falklands debacle (Jaquette 1989: 72–8). Similar women's movements appeared as a response to repressive dictatorships elsewhere, in Chile, Uruguay, El Salvador, and Guatemala (Radcliffe and Westwood 1993: 16–19, 30–64).

Latin American feminist groups drew encouragement from the 'women's liberation' ideology which had appeared in North America and Europe during the 1960s. Diffusion of this new thinking was aided by the rapid gains which women made in higher education and consequently in middle-class, professional employment. Such opportunities were greatly enlarged by the military governments' programmes of technical modernization. For example, female enrolments at Brazil's universities increased five-fold between 1969 and 1975, while that of men only doubled; by 1980 the number of male and female students in the country's universities was roughly equal. Some individuals acquired a heightened feminist consciousness through periods of exile abroad as refugees from political persecution. The United Nations designation of 1975 as International Women's Year, a gesture recognized by several Latin American governments, gave further prominence to the feminist cause (Jaquette 1989: 2–27).

The community groups in which women took a prominent role have already been mentioned (Chapter 4) as examples of the grassroots NSMs seeking the better welfare provision that appeared under military rule, especially in the big city shanty settlements, when political parties and trade unions were closely controlled. These institutions, concerned with national issues and the world of work, had been male dominated, but women were better able to come to the fore in demanding improved health services, schools, or water supplies, matters which related directly to child care and other acknowledged female domestic responsibilities. Women could arrange their household tasks to make time for attending meetings or for lobbying municipal departments during office hours. The mothers' clubs promoted by priests and nuns as part of the Catholic church's parochial work often provided a useful organizational base.

Examples of welfare-related campaigns in which women became conspicuous include the Cost of Living Movements (protesting against inflation) and the Health Movements (to secure neighbourhood medical centres) that appeared in São Paulo and other Brazilian cities during the later years of the military dictatorship. As a response to the 1980s economic crisis women organised communal kitchens in many Latin American shanty town districts, with the aim of counteracting rising food and fuel prices by bulk purchase, and leaving more free time for paid work. The community-based welfare projects favoured by national governments and international agencies since the 1980s (Chapter 5) have particularly tried to encourage women's participation (Roberts 1995: 204–5).

It is argued that these different movements – human rights, feminist, and welfare – developed interconnections, so that women were radicalized and given a stronger sense of common identity through new opportunities for joint action outside their own homes. Acceptance of women's freedom to organize collectively certainly represented a major change in social attitudes. Many middle-class feminists sought to move beyond rarified intellectual discourse by making contact with women in poorer districts. Thus Latin American women became more generally assertive and self-confident, able to push their concerns higher up the political agenda and change aspects of their personal lives. For example, an important feminist principle is the right of women to contraception, so feminist-influenced community movements gave prominence to birth control in their discussion groups and propaganda. Women whose aspirations had been raised by political activism were persuaded of the benefits of smaller families as a way to give themselves and their children greater opportunities (Radcliffe and Westwood 1993: 88–111, 129–30, 148).

However, it is recognized also that the effectiveness of women's mobilizations has been limited in several respects. Argentina's mothers of the Plaza de Mayo, the most notable human rights activists, tried to assure the integrity and moral force of their cause by declaring themselves 'above politics'. They focused exclusively on the issue of their missing children, and would not allow the campaign to be used for broader radical or feminist aims. Yet the mothers failed to sustain their influence after the restoration of democracy, or secure a full investigation of the disappearances. In Argentina and other Latin American countries civilian politicians, with national reconciliation as their main objective, have been concerned not to antagonize the military, and prepared to draw a veil over many of the human rights abuses committed under the dictatorships (Jaquette 1989: 72–94). When the shift back to democracy began, divisions appeared among Latin American feminists between the supporters of rival 'mainstream' male-dominated political parties. Among poorer women there is still a tendency to regard feminism as an alien, upper-class doctrine, and a feeling that politics remains 'men's business' (Jaquette 1989: 46–50). Some mothers' clubs have continued under clerical influence, stressing women's role in home making and child care. While the São Paulo Health Movement has survived, because of the ongoing concern for medical provision, the Crèche Movement, a key element in the feminist programme for emancipating women from domestic work, proved ephemeral. The economic hardship resulting from the debt crisis, and women's need to seek paid work, has left them with less time and energy for community activism (Radcliffe and Westwood 1993: 66–7, 102, 173–96). Men have sometimes moved in to take control of community organizations which have attracted official funding as a result of the shift towards decentralized welfare provision, even when the rank and file membership is mainly female.

Since the early 1980s Latin American governments have been at pains to show their good intentions by establishing new ministries and agencies devoted to women's issues. A number of civil codes have been revised to cut back male privileges in family law, for example regarding divorce and the custody of children. There has been a slight increase in the number of successful female electoral candidates. However, on the whole the practical results from the enhancement of women's political role have been modest, as shown by the failure to protect state welfare spending from the effects of austerity programmes (Chapter 5).

PERSONAL AND FAMILY RELATIONS

A long-standing characteristic of Latin American family structure, at least among the poor, is the custom of unformalized, consensual marriages (*compromisos*). Often these unions are unstable, leading to a high proportion (about 20 per cent) of female-headed households, resulting from male desertions (Bethell 1994a: 23–6). The difficulties faced by such households are another factor aggravating deprivation and inequality. Many of the homeless 'street children' found in Latin American cities come from disrupted families. Family breakdown may have become more common in recent years, though indications on the subject are not very clear (Green 1991: 142; Chant 1991). However, this aspect of Latin American life certainly contrasts with East Asia, where kinship ties are relatively strong at all social levels.

Within this context, to what extent have domestic relations between women and men been modified? The evidence is conflicting. The greater frequency with which women have undertaken paid work may have improved their bargaining position in the family, and allowed mothers to set daughters an example of independent behaviour. Conversely, men's authority may have suffered from the post-1982 decline in their earnings, especially marked for higher-paid formal-sector manual workers. Women as a rule spend a larger proportion of their income than do men on household and children, so perhaps increased female labour force participation has limited the harm done to welfare by the 1980s recession. Political and community activism, whether or not consciously feminist, has broken down the customary exclusion of women from the public domain, given them new sources of information, and increased their self-confidence by bringing them together for mutual support outside the home, often challenging the claims of jealous, suspicious male partners. For example, a woman who has become knowledgeable on the subject is more likely to assert her right to contraception against the objections of a husband who regards numerous children as proof of his virility.

However, women are still confined for the most part to relatively low-paid work, limiting their household budgetary contribution and its effect to the domestic balance of power. When a woman works her husband may reserve more of his own earnings for drink, cigarettes, and other personal expenditure. Some authors imply that the post-1982 economic crisis has affected women even more severely than men. Many of the better female jobs in government welfare services have fallen victim to public spending cuts; the growth of women's employment has been concentrated in street vending and other poorly rewarded informal-sector occupations (Green 1991: 142, 148). Men have shown little inclination to help more at home when their wives go out to work, so Latin American women, with few of the domestic appliances that are generally available in developed countries, must carry an intensified 'double burden' of paid employment and house-hold tasks. (Cuba's radical 1975 Family Code, requiring both marriage partners to share household duties, has not been imitated anywhere else in the region.) Part of the extra burden has fallen on daughters withdrawn from school, at the expense of their future prospects, to assist with housekeeping and the care of younger children, so that mothers can take paid work (Chant 1991: 210–12). One study, of a low-income Ecuador urban neighbourhood, reports an increase during the 1980s of domestic violence against women, caused by economic stresses in those households, still the majority, where the man remains the sole adult breadwinner (Radcliffe and Westwood 1993: 192).

Nevertheless, it must be noted that the available statistics for Latin America as a whole do not yet show any recent deterioration of female life expectancy, either in absolute terms or relative to male standards, though there has been a slight relative decline of girls' school enrolment (Table 6.1). Perhaps the effect of economic hardship in raising women's mortality has been offset by the declining birth rate and the consequently reduced likelihood of death in childbirth.

CONCLUSION

The status of Latin American women has improved over recent decades, a trend with various implications for the region's economic potential, some favourable, and others of more doubtful value. Contraception has become more widespread and birth rates have fallen, broadly matching trends elsewhere, though at a less rapid pace than in East Asia. Slower population growth will make it easier to achieve increases in output per head. Since the 1960s Latin American women have taken an important role in neighbourhood self-help organizations, probably securing some welfare gains and at least mitigating the social costs of the debt crisis. Women's protests against the human rights abuses perpetrated under military rule helped to discredit authoritarian government and consolidate the restored democracies. However, Latin American women's labour force participation has remained comparatively low, partly because employment protection measures have limited female recruitment by manufacturing industry. Heightened feminist consciousness entails extra pressures and demands on elected politicians, possibly interfering with the pursuit of development goals.

7   The natural environment

Relative to its population Latin America is more generously endowed with agricultural land, forests, fresh water, and valuable mineral deposits, than any other Third World region. Nevertheless, since the 1940s the growth of population and economic activity have undoubtedly put pressure on these natural resources. This chapter first examines deforestation, the aspect of Latin American resource depletion that has recently attracted most notice. We then consider some interrelationships between economic and environmental issues. It has been argued that the 1980s debt crisis resulted at least in part from a wasteful use of natural resources, combined with an excessive reliance on capital-, energy-, and chemical-intensive technologies. For example, farmers had become too dependent on imported fertilizers and other petroleum-based agricultural inputs. A lasting recovery can therefore only be achieved if development strategies are put on a 'greener', more 'sustainable', ecologically sensitive basis (Goodman and Redclift 1991; Murray 1994: 136–47). To what extent have Latin America's recent economic problems had environmental causes?

DEFORESTATION

In the early twentieth century about 55–60 per cent of Latin America's surface area was covered by woodland, principally the tropical rain-forests of Central America and the Amazon basin, where sparse indigenous populations continued in more or less complete isolation from 'mainstream' national society. European conquest and settlement had impacted only marginally on the forest zones, through slave raiding against the Amerindians and some missionary efforts. A short-lived boom in the collecting of wild rubber from Amazonia, to supply the developed countries' new bicycle and automobile industries, was brought to an end just before World War I by the establishment of lower-cost plantation production in South East Asia.

Then various influences led to more systematic encroachment on the forests. During the 1930s oil was discovered in the Amazon regions of several Andean countries (Colombia, Ecuador, Peru, Bolivia). The road building that followed to serve the oilfields and assert control over potentially valuable national territory also encouraged some agricultural colonization. The chemical pesticide DDT, invented in 1939, made feasible the control of endemic malaria and other diseases which previously had deterred migration from the *sierra* to the humid tropical lowlands. World War II and the Japanese occupation of South East Asia caused a brief upsurge in the gathering of natural rubber, chicle (then the raw material for chewing gum), and other forest products. As population growth accelerated during the 1940s and 1950s, many Latin American politicians came to see frontier expansion as a social safety valve, a convenient way of making land available for the rural poor and relieving pressure for agrarian reform. The shift away from export dependence associated with ISI apparently required the fuller development of internal resources. This attitude was strikingly expressed by Brazil's relocation of its federal government from Rio de Janeiro 600 miles inland to the new capital city of Brasília, a project begun in 1956.

Brazil's 1964 military coup gave a further impetus to the opening up of the country's Amazon territories. The armed forces had a professional interest in securing the remote western and northern frontiers against foreign penetration. Ambitious road and airfield construction projects advertised the military's organizational competence. Exploitation of the region's natural wealth would help to establish Brazil as a leading world power. Amazonia took an important role in the new regime's plans to increase and diversify the country's exports. It was hoped that forested land could be converted to cattle ranching, a strategy supported for Brazil and other parts of Latin America by development 'experts' and international financial agencies, including the World Bank. Experiments in Australia had shown the possibilities for improving tropical pastures with introduced grass species, mainly of African origin. Modern motor trucks could haul live animals to slaughter over long distances. (Hitherto beef production for export had been concentrated in regions such as the Argentine pampas where there were dense railway networks.) Meat consumption within Latin America was rising strongly, because of income growth. Export prospects for lower-grade beef were good, as a result of the shift of eating habits in the developed countries towards hamburgers and other fast foods.

From the mid-1960s the Brazilian government introduced a system of subsidies and fiscal incentives which particularly favoured large-scale Amazonian cattle ranching. Investment outlays could be set against tax liabilities incurred on business operations elsewhere. Corporate enterprises, many of them based in the industrial southeast, secured extensive land grants, and displaced, often violently, considerable numbers of peasant settlers who had occupied small holdings without legal title. The squatters were pushed further westwards ahead of the capitalist ranching frontier. Settler penetration into Amazonia was helped by government road construction, and the logging trails established to extract timber (Branford and Glock 1985).

During the early 1970s the big business orientation of Brazilian policy was briefly supplemented by programmes for establishing small-scale farmers as colonists along the Trans-Amazon Highway and other newly built roads, to absorb surplus population from the drought-stricken northeastern states. Planners hoped that Amazon development might stem the influx of impoverished rural migrants to the cities. However, the results from officially sponsored settlement based on small farms proved very disappointing, with many of the intended beneficiaries giving up their plots after just a few years. Such schemes failed partly through unfavourable geography. Although the rainforests' luxuriant vegetation gives an appearance of great natural fertility, in fact soil quality is usually low. Adequate crops can be grown for two or three years on newly cleared land, after the tree cover has been felled and burnt. Then yields decline rapidly as nutrients are leached away by tropical rains, and weed infestation takes hold.

These problems might have been eased by more careful planning and management. However, the advance surveys lacked sufficient detail to identify the scattered areas of relatively fertile land, so roads and farms were laid out with little regard for long-term agricultural potential. The extension services providing the settlers with technical advice were cumbersome and understaffed. There were long delays in granting land titles and bank loans. Low construction standards made the new roads impassable for much of the rainy season, limiting farmers' ability to market their crops (Goodman and Hall 1990: 70–8). Perhaps the projects' weak performance was also due partly to the poverty and limited skills of the settlers themselves. Those coming from the northeast, a sugar plantation region, had often been share-croppers or landless estate labourers, with little previous experience in commercial farm management.

A rare instance of prosperous agriculture on the Brazilian rainforest frontier is Tomé-Açú, a settlement founded before World War II by colonists of Japanese origin. They established the cultivation of black pepper for export, the first farmers outside Asia to do so, and then moved into other specialities when the crop began to suffer from disease. Tomé-Açú's success apparently resulted from a strong capacity for cooperative action, which some observers attribute to Japanese cultural values (Goodman and Hall 1990: 366–7).

Official disillusionment with small farmer settlement reinforced the emphasis on large capitalist enterprises as the basis for opening up Brazilian Amazonia, a process that continued at an accelerating pace during the 1970s. A speculative upsurge in land prices gave an extra stimulus to the demand for ranching grants. Brazil's system of estate taxation, assessed at a lower rate on 'improved' acreage, encouraged the rapid conversion of forest to pasture. Corporate business investors, commonly absentees with little farming knowledge, applied unsuitable methods to their newly acquired properties, reducing the chances of long-term agricultural viability. Trees were cleared using heavy tractors which compacted the soil. A perceived disadvantage of more labour-intensive tree-felling with machetes and chainsaws was that workers brought in for the task might seek to remain as squatters. While trying to establish pastures, developers made excessive use of chemical weedkillers, especially the compound Tordon, which included the defoliant 'Agent Orange' employed by the US for removing tree cover in Vietnam. The end of the Vietnam War made available large surplus stocks of Agent Orange during the mid-1970s. Careless herbicide applications killed the nitrogen-fixing leguminous plants required in many areas to complement introduced fodder grasses. So while cattle ranching attracted considerable investments and destroyed extensive rainforest tracts, its productivity was very low (Branford and Glock 1985: 43–81).

Some land grants were developed by private-sector colonization companies, drawing family farmers who had been displaced from coffee growing in southeastern Brazil by the extension of soya beans and other highly mechanized crops. Such enterprises enjoyed rather more success than government schemes, through better management and the selection of relatively prosperous colonists. However, most small farmer settlement was spontaneous, individual, and unplanned. From the late 1970s, as the 'Brazilian miracle' of rapid economic growth faded, industrial recession took hold, and chances of finding work in eastern cities diminished, more of the rural migrant poor sought a livelihood on the Amazon frontier. The attempts of some provincial governors to check colonization became increasingly ineffective as *abertura* weakened the military regime. Surface gold strikes attracted numerous small-scale prospectors and diggers, known as *garimpeiros*. Mining development also occurred on a large-scale capitalist basis, most notably through the undertaking formed to exploit the Carajás iron ore deposits, discovered in 1967. By the mid-1980s the Greater Carajás complex extended over 300,000 square miles, an area as big as Britain and France. It included mines, hydroelectric dams, a 550-mile railway, and associated agricultural colonies. Pig-iron smelters were planned, posing a further threat to the forest through the demand for charcoal as fuel. At the same time improved satellite imagery became available to map changes in land use, indicating how Amazon tree cover was being lost through felling and burning at an accelerating rate, and suggesting that much of the region would be entirely deforested within a few years. The subject attracted widespread media attention in the developed countries. Amazon deforestation, it was argued, would release large quantities of carbon into the atmosphere, and contribute to the recently identified phenomenon of global warming through the 'greenhouse effect' (Branford and Glock 1985: 84–90, 156–8; Goodman and Hall 1990: 136–41, 385–7). There was concern too over the threatened loss of potentially valuable biological species.

The causes of Central American deforestation were broadly similar to those at work in Amazonia, with some distinctive features. From the 1950s there was extensive clearance of forested lowland areas to grow cotton for export, supplementing coffee and bananas, the region's established staples. Commercial cotton production had been made feasible here by the introduction of DDT. The expansion of cattle ranching followed in the 1960s, strongly influenced by the 'hamburger connection' with the US, while traditional *haciendas* began evicting many of their labour tenants as a response to agrarian reform proposals and minimum wage laws. The replacement of ox-draught ploughing by tractors made it possible to conduct agricultural operations with a reduced workforce. Guatemala's military rulers, especially brutal and grasping, enriched themselves through the acquisition of large tracts in the Peten forest region when its oil-bearing potential became clear (Rouquié 1987: 297). Because Central America's industrialization and urbanization were more limited than Brazil's, a larger proportion of the landless poor sought to become established as frontier settlers. Conflict between squatters and encroaching estates developed into widespread guerrilla movements by the 1970s. Much of the road building that accompanied frontier expansion was financed with US aid, provided with an eye to counter-insurgency needs.

ENVIRONMENTAL CONDITIONS AND THE DEBT CRISIS: PROBLEMS OF 'SUSTAINABILITY'?

To what extent have environmental problems been responsible for Latin America's debt crisis of the early 1980s, and the region's subsequent difficulties in achieving a sustained economic recovery? Points made by authors who stress ecological aspects include the wastefulness and the incidental costs of deforestation. Land exposed by the removal of tree cover is subject to rapid erosion. Topsoil loss has been most severe in the Andean countries and Central America, where estate enlargement and the pressure of rural population growth have pushed peasant cultivators up steep mountain slopes. As well as degrading the newly cleared land, hill wash causes silt to accumulate in reservoirs, reducing the capacity of hydroelectric and irrigation facilities. Also, because forest canopy holds moisture and contributes to rainfall by releasing water vapour, deforestation increases the likelihood of drought. For example, Ecuador takes 60 per cent of its electricity supplies from a single hydroelectric scheme. In 1995 the country suffered its worst power cuts for thirty years, through drought combined with sedimentation. In Panama, where the share of land under forest has declined from 70 per cent to 30 per cent since 1945, lower rainfall threatens the viability of the trans-isthmian canal, a crucial revenue source (Green 1991: 37–43).

Another topic attracting notice is the damage caused by pesticides. This problem became most conspicuous in Central America, where the post-1945 extension of cotton cultivation over the coastal plains depended on DDT applications against boll weevils and malarial mosquitoes. Technical support came from North American chemical companies, and agricultural supply firms based in the southern US cotton-growing states. Central American conditions – geographically concentrated monocropping, high humidity, and the absence of winter frosts (unlike the US south) – made pest control especially difficult. Therefore growers responded with heavier pesticide usage, insect strains quickly built up resistance, and applications had to be repeated ever more frequently, as often as forty or fifty times a year. On this 'pesticide treadmill' chemical inputs accounted for more than a third of cotton production costs in Guatemala, El Salvador, and Nicaragua by the late 1970s. Indiscriminate aerial spraying made pesticide poisoning a serious public health problem. Breast milk samples from women in Central American cotton-growing districts show some of the highest levels of DDT ever recorded in human populations (World Bank 1992: 140). Soil erosion from deforested land combined with pesticide runoff to degrade waterways, mangrove swamps, and coastal fisheries. Central American cotton growing itself became uneconomic in the early 1980s, when crop prices fell, and devaluations raised the cost of imported chemicals. The region's cotton exports have subsequently dwindled to insignificance (Murray 1994).

Mexico City provides the most striking case within Latin America of urban environmental problems. The city lies at an altitude of 6,000–7,000 feet on Mexico's central plateau, in a valley basin encircled by mountains. This site, the focal point of the pre-conquest Aztec empire, was taken by the Spanish in the sixteenth century for a colonial capital, to secure control over the subjugated Indians. Under ISI the Mexico City region came by the 1980s to account for about a quarter of the country's population, and nearly half of its income, industrial output, and automobile ownership. This represents the common Latin American pattern, with twentieth-century urbanization markedly concentrated in a single 'primate' city, usually the nation's capital. Mexico City's inhabitants now number almost twenty million. Urban growth on such a scale, in such a location, has generated severe atmospheric pollution from industrial plant and motor vehicles, their engine efficiency impaired by the high altitude. Dust blown from deforested hillsides is added to the smoke and exhaust fumes. Temperature inversions often trap the contaminated air within the valley basin. Apart from the human suffering and economic burden caused by the growing incidence of lung disease, corrective measures attempted since the debt crisis have required the closure of many factories (Gilbert 1994: 120). Subsidence resulting from the extraction of underground water reserves aggravated the damage caused by the 1985 earthquake. The cost of meeting the city's water demands is rising sharply, because of the need to pump in additional supplies over long distances, across mountain terrain.

The Chilean capital Santiago, with a similar mountain valley geography, has also experienced chronic air pollution, made worse by an ill-judged neoliberal deregulation of bus transport implemented under the Pinochet dictatorship. The reform caused underused services to proliferate, employing large numbers of aged, second-hand imported vehicles (Collins and Lear 1995: 231–42).

However, although these instances of economic loss through ecological damage may have local significance, the extent to which they represent a more general Latin American environmental crisis is doubtful. The pesticide-related collapse of cotton growing which occurred during the 1980s was peculiar to Central America. Cotton output held steady in South America, while over Latin America as a whole the production of bananas, another crop that involves heavy pesticide applications, rose strongly (FAO 1995: 166, 182). Since the debt crisis several Caribbean basin countries have tried to improve their foreign trade position by growing 'non-traditional' fruit and vegetables (melons, pineapples, strawberries, broccoli, etc.) for sale to the developed world. Fruit exports have made an important contribution to Chile's economic recovery. It has been argued that because these new lines also depend on chemical pest control, they will give rise to the same environmental and public health difficulties as did cotton (Murray 1994: 56–97). However, importing countries subject horticultural products, items for human consumption, to strict quality controls. Shipments found with high chemical residue levels are excluded, obliging growers to exercise more restraint in their use of pesticides.

Recent trends in urban air quality are not wholly unfavourable. Mexico City and Santiago have certainly experienced serious problems, but they result to a large extent from distinctive local geography. In other conurbations, for example the Brazilian city of São Paulo, Latin America's most important centre of manufacturing industry, air pollution has been falling. In the developed countries public concern aroused during the 1960s over environmental standards led to the tighter regulation of emission levels, and new technologies for pollution control. These technologies have since become more widely available, to make possible the improvement of conditions in 'middle income' Latin America. The worst urban air pollution now occurs in 'low income' countries, such as India and China (World Bank 1992: 50–3, 199). The measures taken by the Chilean government since 1990, enforcing the withdrawal of older buses and their replacement by updated models, offers a way to cut drastically air contamination from exhaust fumes in Santiago (Hojman 1993: 140–1). During the last fifteen years Latin American urban growth has slackened, and become more widely dispersed over a range of provincial towns, rather than being concentrated in a few unwieldy primate cities (Roberts 1995: 90–1, 208). These changes are partly due to the turn away from state-led ISI.

Care must also be taken to avoid sweeping generalizations on the subject of forest clearance. The process has certainly been very rapid in Central America, reducing the wooded area at an annual rate of 2 or 3 per cent, and causing considerable incidental damage (World Bank 1996: 206–7). Population densities here are quite high, so land hunger among the rural poor and the need for increased agricultural exports to service foreign debt have kept up the momentum of deforestation (Goodman and Redclift 1991: 184–204). However, in Brazilian

Amazonia, which accounts for more than half of Latin America's forested area, the situation now seems to be rather less ominous than was once supposed. During the mid-1980s published assessments indicated that about 23,200 square miles of rainforest were being lost each year, a 1.8 per cent annual depletion rate (Goodman and Hall 1990: 386). Estimates of the annual loss were subsequently revised downwards to 8,100 square miles (0.6 per cent) for the 1978–88 period, and during the later 1980s the clearance rate fell, reaching 5,300 square miles (0.4 per cent) in 1990 (World Bank 1993: 323).

There are several reasons why the pace of Brazilian deforestation has eased. When criticism of the 'assault on the Amazon' first began to appear in the developed world, reactions from Brazil were predominantly hostile. Environmentalism was represented, especially by the military, landowners, and big business, as an 'imperialist' First World doctrine, propagated with the aim of shackling the country's development. However, groups under threat from development projects – rubber tappers, small farmers, *garimpeiros*, forest Indians – had been evolving organized forms of collective resistance and self-defence during the later years of military rule. Amazon grassroots mobilizations of the NSM type gained extra strength by establishing contact with foreign conservationist NGOs. For example, in 1987 Chico Mendes, a rubber tappers' leader, drew attention to their cause on a highly successful visit to the US. The following year he was murdered at the instigation of landowners opposed to his campaign for establishing a forest reserve. This much-publicized killing caused outrage both within Brazil and abroad (Green 1991: 41–2; Goodman and Redclift 1991: 117–18). Many Indian peoples also drew encouragement from NGO activists and the end of authoritarian rule to mount impressive campaigns in defence of their traditional lands (Cubitt 1995: 70–9). The environmentalist cause gained support from a broader range of Brazilian anti-elite opinion and became a significant force in national politics.

Lobbying by US environmentalists concerned about global warming, an issue given extra prominence by the drought that affected North America in 1988, obliged the World Bank to cut funding for projects, such as dam building and road asphalting, that might encourage deforestation. Political circumstances and financial constraints forced the Brazilian government to end its subsidies for the establishment of new cattle ranches. Some progress has been made through research and experiment on methods of upgrading older, low-quality pastures, as an alternative to further land clearance (National Research Council 1993: 316–18). From the later 1980s migration into

Amazonia by poor settlers and fortune seekers also declined. The federal government no longer had the resources for initiating major new highway construction schemes. Inadequate maintenance allowed many stretches of the trunk roads built during the 1960s and 1970s to become impassable and overgrown. A modest revival of industrial activity improved employment prospects elsewhere. Gold strikes became less frequent; most of the surface deposits accessible to *garimpeiros* are now probably exhausted.

Nevertheless, powerful forces are still at work encroaching on the forest. While the capacity of the federal government for promoting development has been curtailed, Brazil's new constitution, enacted in 1988, gives individual states greater autonomy and a larger share of tax revenues. Territories formerly under federal administration have been granted statehood for the first time. Amazon state governors are anxious to please their constituents, for example by building feeder roads that open up new areas for settlement. Immigration has declined, but local population growth through natural increase continues. There has been no significant agrarian reform to reduce inequalities in landownership. Much of the growth in cattle ranching involves smaller herds, whose owners never received subsidies and are not affected by the loss of public support. Because credit is now scarce and expensive, ranchers upgrading their pastures commonly dispose of their remaining timber reserves to obtain finance. Very little has been done to establish more sustainable agricultural practices among small settlers, by technical assistance and the granting of secure property titles. During the 1980s underfunding and greater politicization impaired the effectiveness of research institutions concerned with agricultural development in Amazonia (National Research Council 1993: 309, 318–42). An implicit subsidy for extensive development remains through the practice of *Petrobrás*, the federal government's monopoly petroleum enterprise, in maintaining uniform motor vehicle fuel prices throughout Brazil, without regard to transport costs.

So land clearance continues. On current trends about 10 per cent of the Brazilian rainforest will have been destroyed by the year 2000 and about 40 per cent by the middle of the next century. This may accelerate global warming and deprive humanity of valuable biological species. It will certainly threaten many of the surviving indigenous forest peoples. However, environmental degradation, even if undesirable in itself, is not yet a major constraint on the Brazilian economy as a whole. For example, the threat of power shortages currently faced by the country's manufacturing industry results from the financial difficulties that have prevented the completion of many hydroelectric schemes begun before the debt crisis, rather than from soil erosion and reservoir sedimentation. The energy problem could be resolved for the time being by the more effective mobilization of capital, from either domestic or international sources. Similar points apply to Brazil's South American neighbours, where natural resources remain abundant, except for the densely populated highland regions of Bolivia, Peru, and Ecuador. Forests still cover about 46 per cent of Latin America's land area: 58 per cent in Brazil, 48 per cent in South America as a whole, but only 28 per cent in Mexico and Central America (FAO 1995: 6–8).

CONCLUSION

Latin American deforestation accelerated between the 1930s and the 1970s, as a result of population growth and new economic opportunities. By the 1980s the loss of forest cover was giving rise to widespread concern. Other notable environmental issues include the overuse of agricultural pesticides and urban air pollution. However, Latin America's natural resources are relatively abundant, so it is unlikely that ecological degradation has been an important cause of the region's recent economic difficulties, except in Central America and parts of the Andean highlands. To what extent can grassroots mobilization provide a defence against pressures on the environment? Popular movements have helped to check some large-scale Amazonian development projects, and thus slow down the rate of deforestation, since the mid-1980s. Nevertheless, it is doubtful whether joint action by the poor will be able to play a more positive, constructive role over the longer term. 'Social forestry' initiatives, making local communities responsible for woodland management, have shown some promise as a conservation strategy in South and East Asia, where there are long traditions of stable peasant village life. However, in Latin America several centuries of estate domination have left most of the rural population with few firm collective ties or identities. Successful co-operation among rainforest settlers to solve technical problems and achieve agricultural sustainability, as exemplified by the Japanese colonists of Tomé-Açú, remains rare.

8 Latin America in the 1990s
Problems and potential

What are Latin America's current prospects? It is of course impossible to predict with any confidence, especially bearing in mind the region's record of instability and unexpected misfortunes. Table 8.1 presents various economic statistics relating to Latin America since 1991, together with comparable data for the years 1983–90, the period following the onset of the debt crisis. The early 1990s brought a resumption of large capital inflows to the region (Chapter 2). At the same time the burden of interest charges on foreign loans was eased, through the general fall of interest rates in developed country money markets, and the relief provided under the Brady plan for debt restructuring (Chapter 3). These developments have reversed the net transfer of resources from Latin America that occurred during the later 1980s. The growth of Latin American export earnings has quickened, and there have been some small gains in output per head.

We therefore begin by reviewing further how Latin America has recently benefited from improved external circumstances, and might perhaps continue to do so. The data in Table 8.1 are intended to emphasize that the net resource transfer to Latin America since 1991 is quite modest relative to regional output. The inflow has been accompanied by a decline in Latin America's own savings rate, and has brought only a slight growth in investment. These are important aspects of the continuing structural weaknesses noted in the chapter's final section.

ECONOMIC DEVELOPMENT: AN IMPROVING INTERNATIONAL CONTEXT?

Chapter 2 examined the early results from programmes of economic liberalization. Tariff cuts, financial deregulation, and the privatization of state enterprises, have so far failed to generate rapid export-led

Table 8.1 Economic trends in Latin America, 1983–95

	Annual growth of output per head (%)	Annual growth of exports (%)	Annual net capital inflows (billion US$)	Share of GDP (%)				
				Net capital inflows	Payments abroad of interest and profits	Resource transfer to (+) or from the region	Regional investment rate	Regional savings rate
	(1)	(2)	(3)	(4)	(5)	(6)*	(7)	(8)
1983—90	nil	4.0	15.0	1.3	4.1	-2.8	18.0	21.0
1991—95	1.2	9.1	48.0	3.3	2.3	+1.0	20.0	19.0

Note: * Column (6) is roughly equivalent to column (4) minus (5), and to column (7) minus (8)

Sources Estimated from Bethell 1994a: 228, 241, 245; IMF 1996; World Bank 1990–6

manufacturing growth along East Asian lines. Neoliberal prescriptions underestimate the extent to which East Asian industrialization involved state support. They rest on an excessively doctrinaire faith in the benefits likely to come from the free play of market forces. Since the early 1980s East Asia has strengthened its position as the main source of Third World manufactured exports, not through following neoliberal recommendations, but through the spread of industrialization from Japan and the 'Gang of Four' to Malaysia, Thailand, Indonesia, and, above all, China. In these 'follower' countries enormous local reserves of cheap labour are being combined with capital, management, and technology provided by the region's 'leader' economies.

Factory wage rates in China are still only about a quarter of those paid in Latin America. Therefore it is most unlikely that the restructuring and efficiency gains stimulated by liberalization will establish the region as a major force in world markets for the labour-intensive manufactures of the type on which industrial exporters have usually relied in the early stages of development. Indeed, in several Latin American countries the recent dismantling of ISI trade barriers has caused textiles production and other 'light' industries to contract, under pressure from cheaper Asian imports.

The best opportunities for Latin American export manufacturing are to be found in Mexico and the smaller Caribbean basin republics, which have the benefit of close proximity to the US market. Mexico has reinforced its locational advantage by joining with the US and Canada in the 1993 North American Free-Trade Agreement (NAFTA), a treaty to eliminate tariff barriers between the three countries. Washington promoted NAFTA with the aim of securing Mexico's political stability and commitment to economic liberalization; Mexican manufactured exports have certainly grown rapidly as a result. Nevertheless, the US administration had difficulty in getting the treaty ratified by Congress, because of concern over the threat posed by low-cost Mexican labour to employment in US industries. So there is little chance in the foreseeable future of the agreement being extended to include other Latin American countries, seen by Washington as less strategically important.

They have been left to construct their own free trade areas, for example *Mercosur*, established in 1991 by Brazil, Argentina, Uruguay, and Paraguay. Such arrangements have had some stimulating effects. The wider regional market opportunities offered by *Mercosur* encouraged several foreign automobile companies to enlarge and refurbish their Brazilian manufacturing operations, stagnant since the early 1980s. However, economic integration between neighbouring countries is being limited by poor transport infrastructure and the failure to develop common institutions. The share of intraregional exports in Latin American trade has not yet recovered to the levels achieved in the 1970s.

While the immediate prospects for Latin America's manufactured exports and interregional trade are on the whole rather limited, the region does have useful advantages as a source of primary commodities. Over the last fifteen years continuing rapid industrialization and income growth have greatly enlarged East Asia's appetite for imported food, metals, fuels, and timber products. As a result, commodity markets have been quite buoyant in the 1990s, despite the recession that affected most developed countries during the early part of the decade. This contrasts with the collapse of raw material prices associated with the 1982 debt crisis.

Latin America is quite well placed to profit from the renewed resilience of international commodity trade. Budget imbalances are making the US and Western European countries less willing to support their own farmers and farm exports with the government subsidies that have depressed the price of agricultural goods on world markets for much of the post-World War II period. Latin America still has a relatively generous endowment of farm land, not yet lost through environmental degradation (Chapter 7). Several countries in the region, Brazil most notably, have maintained strong agricultural research programmes (Maddison *et al.* 1992: 67; ECLAC 1992: 65), offering the means to improve cultivation methods, at least on capitalist estates.

Latin America also contains a large proportion of the world's mineral deposits. During the ISI period their exploitation was held back by nationalist hostility to outside investment in the sector, a reaction against the earlier 'imperialist' abuses of foreign firms. By the 1970s expropriations and punitive taxation had largely excluded international oil and mining corporations from the region, obliging them to concentrate their activities in more politically favourable areas, for example North America and Australia. Since the late 1980s, liberalization programmes have allowed foreign mining companies back into Latin America, with improved prospecting and recovery technologies, and without the management inefficiencies that characterize indigenous state enterprises. The new projects currently under way should yield an enlarged stream of exports in the next few years (Hojman 1993: 143–7).

Latin America is also continuing to attract a broader range of foreign investors. In 1993 annual capital inflows reached US $65 billion. Then events in Mexico threatened to precipitate a renewed financial crisis (Chapter 2). However, external funding has continued on a substantial scale, totalling $47 billion in 1994 and $62 billion in 1995. Mexico's problems have not yet brought the 'repeat of the debt crisis of the early 1980s' anticipated by some commentators (Green 1995: 87). Several influences have helped to maintain confidence at a higher level in the 1990s than in the 1980s. These include Latin America's improved export performance, and the commitment shown by most governments to neoliberal reform. As a contrast, the 1982 crisis was followed by a phase of erratic policy, before the neoliberal approach became generally established. Considerable progress has been made in strengthening public revenues, eliminating budget deficits, and curbing inflation.

Latin American elites have taken comfort from the macroeconomic improvements to repatriate some of their flight capital. These holdings constitute, potentially at least, a most valuable reserve for financing renewed development. Regulatory reform in the US has given the country's insurance companies and mutual funds (unit trusts) greater freedom to put their assets into foreign bonds and shares, including those issued from developing countries. The major investment firms have set up Latin American research departments to monitor the region's risks and opportunities, making capital flows less volatile than the ill-informed, over-optimistic bank lending that led to the 1982 debt crisis. During the 1980s monetary authorities in the developed countries, their attitudes shaped by memories of the inflation-ridden 1970s, kept interest rates high. In the 1990s official fear of inflation has abated, interest rates have been allowed to fall, and the more modest yields available in First World money markets have encouraged investors to seek better returns elsewhere. After the 1989–90 collapse of communism in the Soviet Union and Eastern Europe it was thought for a time that economic reconstruction there might attract large amounts of foreign capital. However, political uncertainties in the former Soviet Union have limited its ability to absorb external finance. All these circumstances are helping to renew Latin America's appeal as an outlet for international investment. Latin Americans have apparently turned away from the populist and ISI delusions of the 1945–80 period, while foreign lenders have learned to exercise greater vigilance over the use made of their money. Perhaps this will ensure that capital is employed more efficiently and intelligently than in the past.

SOME CONTINUING STRUCTURAL WEAKNESSES

Nevertheless, Latin America is still beset by many problems, which make the limited economic gains achieved over the last few years highly insecure. The debt crisis has been alleviated by renewed capital inflows, expressing the First World money markets' endorsement of neoliberal policies. But will this confidence prove well founded? The first stages of liberalization, all that most countries have traversed so far, are in certain respects quite straightforward. The key elements – cutting protective tariff duties, curbing government expenditure, restricting the money supply to bring down inflation, beginning the privatization of state enterprises – are technically simple. They can usually be implemented as executive decisions by national presidents, ministers of finance, and central bank governors. However, the additional 'microeconomic' reforms needed to make capitalism function efficiently over the longer term are likely to prove much more difficult. They often entail complex new laws which must be carried through elected assemblies, in the face of entrenched vested interests. Competent bureaucracies are required to draft and administer legislation. These points may be illustrated through the issue of domestic resource mobilization, taking Chile, the most plausible example of successful neoliberalism, as a special case.

It was noted earlier (Table 8.1) that the annual net resource transfer to Latin America is still very small as a proportion of regional output. Most of the extra capital investment needed for establishing economic growth on a solid basis will have to be financed from an increase of local savings. This has been achieved by Chile, where the savings rate rose from 20 per cent of GDP in 1980 to 23 per cent in 1990, and

28 per cent in 1994. But the corresponding figures for Latin America as a whole are 23 per cent, 22 per cent, and 20 per cent. In the East Asian NICs savings and investment rates run at 30–40 per cent of GDP (World Bank 1992: 235; World Bank 1996: 213). It is widely considered that much of the Chilean improvement has come through the country's reformed pension funds (Chapter 5), so several other Latin American countries are now trying to adapt their pension systems along similar lines, with IMF and World Bank encouragement. However, the general feasibility of this approach remains open to question. The Chilean reform in its early stages devalued most existing pensions rights and left a larger share of the population without any entitlement, steps which could be taken by a firmly entrenched military dictatorship. Latin America's restored democracies must now take fuller account of public opinion, including pensioners, a numerous and formidable interest group. Thus Brazil's new 1988 Constitution promised a massive enlargement of welfare benefits, without providing the means to pay for them (Bethell 1994b: 79–81). Since his election in 1995 President Cardoso has experienced great difficulty in persuading the Brazilian Congress to strengthen the public finances by enacting a pensions reform.

Shortly after they were established some of Chile's *AFP*s became insolvent as a result of careless investments and had to be taken into temporary state ownership. However, they were soon reprivatized, under the oversight of a newly created official superintending agency, which has ensured prudent management ever since. During the later 1980s the system's legitimacy was strengthened by the high yields which the *AFP*s began to secure for their participants, through the acquisition on generous terms of shares in divested state enterprises. Privatization took on an element of 'popular capitalism' (Hojman 1993: 132–7). New regulations established a more competitive banking structure which, together with the invigorated national stock market, allowed smaller firms to secure finance on reasonable terms. Elsewhere in Latin America, however, privatization has been less carefully managed, commonly serving to enrich a few well-connected individuals. State subsidies are being used in a corrupt fashion to shore up oligopolistic banking networks.

The Chilean experience indicates that a strengthened economic performance through neoliberal measures still requires capable government, if only in a regulatory, supervisory function, to ensure a suitable institutional environment for capitalist enterprise. It is not enough for the state simply to withdraw and allow market forces free play. However, government administrative competence has been historically low in most of Latin America (Chapter 4), and since the debt crisis the declining real value of public employees' pay has given them further encouragement to engage in corrupt practices (Bethell 1994a: 45).

Education is another area in which the state must clearly take an active role, and here too Chile stands apart from its neighbours. It is the only country in the region which has made any real attempt at correcting the bias of public outlays towards the university sector (Chapter 5). In the rest of Latin America educational bureaucracies remain notoriously negligent and overstaffed. Elementary and secondary enrolment levels may have continued to rise, but the trend, accompanied by reduced government spending, has almost certainly brought a fall in standards, through the deterioration of school buildings, shortages of teaching materials, and teachers' demoralization. Latin America's disadvantage relative to East Asia in education and human capital is still widening.

Only limited benefits are to be expected from grassroots activism in improving social services and infrastructure, suggestions of the post-modernist left notwithstanding. Experience shows that for 'bottom up' initiatives to flourish, they must have firm 'top down' coordination, provided by well-run government agencies.

So far Latin Americans have on the whole accepted the hardships resulting from the debt crisis and subsequent adjustments with remarkable fortitude, bringing a measure of equilibrium to the region's politics (Chapter 4). However, it would be rash to assume that this will continue for long, if neoliberal policies do not succeed soon in bringing greater economic benefits, shared with greater equity. Traditions of radical popular insurgency, although weakened, are by no means dead, as shown for example by the persistence of southern Mexico's Zapatista uprising since 1994. The only important item of material consumption that has spread more widely in Latin America over recent years is television ownership, offering poorer viewers tantalizing glimpses of the affluence enjoyed by the developed world and by national elites (ECLAC 1992: 24–8). At the same time recession has closed off the opportunities for individual upward mobility into higher-status occupations that helped to limit popular discontent during the ISI period, while the scope for 'Bismarckian' social control through cooption and patronage has been eroded by the contraction of resources at the state's disposal (Roberts 1995: 156, 197–207). Unless the region's deep-seated problems of misgovernment and inequality are addressed, then there is a strong likelihood that Latin America's modest economic recovery will be brought to a halt by renewed cycles of political instability and conflict.

Appendix
Chronology

1492	Christopher Columbus reaches the Caribbean.
1500	Portuguese sailors reach Brazil.
1810–25	All the mainland Latin American colonies gain independence.
1823	US President James Monroe's declaration against any further attempts by European powers to extend their political presence in the Americas (the 'Monroe doctrine').
1910–20	Mexico: revolution and civil war.
1914–18	World War I
1929	US stock market crash leads to world-wide economic depression, and the collapse of Latin American export earnings.
1930	Brazil: military coup overthrows elite-dominated 'Old Republic'; Getúlio Vargas becomes president.
1930–2	Military coups provoked by economic crisis in several other Latin American countries.
1941	US enters World War II. All Latin American countries eventually break relations with the Axis powers and ally themselves with the US.
1945	End of World War II.
1946	Deteriorating US–Soviet relations; onset of the cold war. Argentina: Juan Perón elected president.
1947	Mutual defence treaty (the 'Rio Pact') between US and Latin American states.
1948	Founding of the ECLA. Peru, Venezuela: military coups establish conservative dictatorships. Colombia: assassination of the populist politician Jorge Gaitán leads to destructive riots in the capital Bogotá, and *La Violencia*, several years of civil war in the countryside.
1950	Brazil: Vargas elected president on a populist platform.

1951   Argentina: Perón re-elected president.
1952   Bolivia: revolution against the 'traditional' elite of hacienda and tin mine owners. Argentina: death of Eva Perón.
1953   Dwight D. Eisenhower takes office as US president. End of the Korean War initiates a long-term decline in the price of Latin American raw material exports.
1954   Guatemala: US-backed rebellion overthrows the reformist government of Jacobo Arbenz. Brazil: economic and political crisis; President Vargas commits suicide. Mexico: devaluation of the peso temporarily re-establishes export competitiveness.
1955   Argentina: Perón ousted from the presidency by a military coup.
1956   Brazil: the populist Juscelino Kubitscheck takes office as president, launches ambitious new ISI schemes and the construction of Brasília.
1958   Venezuela: overthrow of military dictator Pérez Jiménez. Chile: IMF-backed austerity measures provoke a political crisis. Colombia: power-sharing agreement between the two main political parties.
1959   Cuban revolution: Fidel Castro overthrows the dictator Batista, establishes a socialist regime, and breaks with the US.
1961   John F. Kennedy takes office as US president; announces the US-funded 'Alliance for Progress', to promote economic development and social reform in Latin America.
1962   Cuban missile crisis: US naval blockade against Cuba to secure the removal of Soviet nuclear missiles.
1963   Peru: election of reformist Belaúnde Terry as president. Lyndon Johnson succeeds Kennedy as US president.
1964   Brazil: 'bureaucratic-authoritarian' military coup. Chile: election of reformist Eduardo Frei as president.
1965   Dominican Republic: invasion by US forces.
1966   Argentina: 'bureaucratic-authoritarian' military coup.
1967   Bolivia: Ché Guevara, associate of Fidel Castro, killed by security forces while trying to instigate Cuban-style rural guerrilla movement.
1968   Panama, Peru: radical-reformist military coups. Mexico: security forces kill several hundred student demonstrators in Mexico City.
1969   Richard Nixon takes office as US president. Argentina: riots

in the city of Córdoba weaken the military government's authority. Bolivia: military coup.

1970   Chile: Salvador Allende, a Marxist, elected president. Mexico: Luis Echeverría elected president, policy becomes more populist and expansionary.

1972   Argentina: Juan Perón returns from exile. Ecuador: military coup. Nixon re-elected US president.

1973   Arab–Israeli War and OPEC action leads to four-fold oil price increase. Latin America's foreign debt US $40 billion. Chile: military coup, death of Allende, establishment of military dictatorship under General Augusto Pinochet. Argentina: Perón elected president.

1974   Argentina: death of Perón. Nixon's resignation from US presidency, succeeded by Gerald Ford.

1976   Argentina: military coup.

1977   Jimmy Carter takes office as US president.

1978   Panama: agreement of revised Canal treaty with US.

1979   Nicaragua: overthrow of dictator Anastasio Somoza by Sandinista revolutionaries.

1980   Peru: military junta relinquishes power. El Salvador: murder of reformist Archbishop Oscar Romero by a right-wing assassin.

1981   Ronald Reagan takes office as US president, backs Contras' campaign against the Sandinista government in Nicaragua.

1982   Argentina occupies the Falkland Islands (Islas Malvinas), a British colony. The islands are then retaken by a British task-force. Mexico: the government's declaration that it cannot meet interest payments on foreign borrowing precipitates the debt crisis. Latin American foreign debt US $331 billion.

1983   Grenada: invasion by US forces to overthrow radical government. Argentina: military government relinquishes power.

1985   'Baker plan' for Latin American debt relief. Brazil: military government relinquishes power. Peru: Alan García elected president, embarks on expansionary populist economic programme. Argentina: unsuccessful 'austral plan' for inflation control.

1986   Brazil: unsuccessful 'cruzado plan' for inflation control.

1988   Mexico: Carlos Salinas de Gortari elected president, continues neoliberal economic policies. Chile: plebiscite vote against allowing Pinochet a further presidential term. Brazil: revised constitution devolves power from the federal government to states and municipalities, and promises increased social benefits.

1989   George Bush takes office as US president. Brazil: Fernando Collor de Mello elected president, defeating the left-wing candidate Luis Inácio ('Lula') da Silva. Panama: US invasion, capture of dictator General Manuel Noriega to stand trial in US on drugs charges. Argentina: Carlos Menem, the Peronist party candidate, elected president, implements neoliberal economic policies. Chile: Patricio Aylwin elected president to succeed Pinochet. Venezuela: more than 300 killed in riots against IMF-prescribed austerity measures. 'Brady plan' for Latin American debt relief. Annual inflation rate 4,900 per cent in Argentina; 1,860 per cent in Brazil; 2,780 per cent in Peru; 20 per cent in Mexico; 21 per cent in Chile.

1990   Peru: Alberto Fujimori elected president, implements neoliberal economic policies. Nicaragua: Violeta Chamorro elected president, Sandinistas relinquish office.

1991   Resumption of large-scale capital inflows to Latin America, for the first time since 1982. Every country in the region except Cuba has an elected president.

1992   Brazil: President Collor de Mello impeached on corruption charges. Peru: President Fujimori dissolves Congress and suspends constitution; arrest of Abimael Guzmán, leader of the *Sendero Luminoso* guerrilla movement. El Salvador: agreement with FMLN guerrillas ends twelve years of civil war.

1993   Bill Clinton takes office as US president. Colombia: security forces kill Pablo Escobar, a leading member of the Medellín drugs 'cartel'. Annual net private capital inflows to Latin America reach US $65 billion.

1994   Mexico: 'Zapatista' uprising in the southern state of Chiapas; political and economic uncertainties check capital inflows; Ernesto Zedillo elected president; peso devalued. Brazil: 'real plan' of finance minister Fernando Henrique Cardoso reduces inflation; Cardoso elected president, defeating 'Lula' da Silva. Venezuela: Rafael Caldera elected president on a populist, anti-neoliberal platform.

1995   Mexico: new austerity measures and severe economic recession; US $50 billion international support scheme for the peso. Argentina: Menem re-elected president, economic recession. Peru: Fujimori re-elected president. Latin

American output per head falls by 0.7 per cent, after growing 3.1 per cent in 1994. Net capital inflows to the region total US $62 billion.

1996   Mexico: economic recovery, stock market reaches record high. Argentina: economic recovery, dismissal of finance minister Domingo Caballo, architect of stabilization measures. Brazil: accelerated privatization programme, government rescue of insolvent banks. Annual inflation rates: Argentina nil; Brazil 11 per cent; Mexico 28 per cent; Chile 7 per cent. Estimated growth of Latin American output per head: 2.0 per cent.

Glossary

abertura	'Opening': the partial relaxation of authoritarian rule and return to electoral politics allowed by the military regime in Brazil from the late 1970s.
AFPs	*Administradoras de Fondos de Previsión* (or *Pensiones*). The privately managed contributory pension funds established in Chile from 1979.
balance of payments	The balance between a country's inflows and outflows of foreign exchange. An excess of outflows over inflows constitutes a balance of payments deficit.
bond	A fixed-interest security or loan instrument.
bureaucratic/ authoritarian	Term applied to Latin American military authoritarian regimes established during the 1960s, especially in Brazil and Argentina, dedicated to securing social 'order' and economic development.
caudillo	A national military dictator or regional leader, especially characteristic of ex-Spanish American territories in the nineteenth century.
Creole	American-born person of European descent.
devaluation	See overvaluation.
ECLA(C)	Economic Commission for Latin America (and the Caribbean). A United Nations agency, based in Santiago, Chile.
garimpeiro	(Brazil) Small-scale 'informal-sector' gold prospector and miner.
GDP	Gross domestic product. A measure of national output.

GNP	Gross national product. An alternative measure of national output.
hacienda	A large landed estate.
IMF	International Monetary Fund. An international agency based in Washington, D.C.. Provides short- and medium-term loans to countries with balance of payments difficulties, usually on condition that macroeconomic policy is changed.
informal sector	Small-scale industrial or service activity, usually conducted by self-employed individuals (for example street vendors), with very little capital, outside formal government regulations concerning tax payments, social security contributions, minimum wages, and safety standards.
ISI	Import substituting industrialization.
LDC	Less developed country.
Liberation Theology	Reformist doctrine, stressing the need to achieve social justice, that became influential in the Roman Catholic church during the 1960s and 1970s.
macroeconomic	Relating to national economic aggregates, such as the balance of payments, inflation, government spending, and revenue.
maquiladoras	Export-oriented assembly plants established in Mexico along the US border.
Mercosur	'Market of the South'. Regional trade agreement concluded in 1991 between Brazil, Argentina, Paraguay, and Uruguay.
mestizo	Person of mixed European and Indian descent.
microeconomic	Detailed aspects of economic behaviour, structure, and policy, for example educational provision, or government regulation of business.
MNC	Multinational corporation. A large capitalist enterprise, operating in several countries.
mulatto	Person of mixed African and European descent.
NAFTA	North American Free Trade Agreement,

concluded in 1993 between the US, Canada, and Mexico.

NGO   Non-government organization.

NIC   Newly industrialized country.

NSM   New social movement. Popular movement, of the type that became common under military rule during the 1970s; in general locally based, and concerned with social welfare or human rights issues.

oligopoly   A small number of firms in a particular sector, able to collude and restrict competition.

OPEC   Organization of Petroleum Exporting Countries.

overvaluation   A national currency is said to be overvalued when its rate of exchange with other currencies makes the country's exports uncompetitive abroad, and imported goods relatively cheap. Consequently balance of payments deficits become unsustainably large. In Latin America since 1945 overvaluation has most commonly occurred as a result of domestic price inflation continuing at a relatively high rate by international standards. For example, during the period from 1970 to 1976 the official exchange rate between the Mexican peso and the US dollar remained unchanged at 12.5 pesos = $1, while annual inflation averaged about 15 per cent in Mexico but only 7 per cent in the US. This stability of the nominal exchange rate, despite the difference in inflation levels, entailed a rise or appreciation of Mexico's real effective exchange rate (REER) relative to the US, the country's principal trading partner. Mexican exports and foreign exchange earnings were limited by the increasing overvaluation of the peso. Overvaluation can be corrected by lowering the exchange rate through a devaluation. For example, in 1976–7 the Mexican peso was devalued from 12.5 to about 22.7 pesos = US $1. Devaluing may make a country's exports cheaper and more attractive to foreign buyers. However, the adjustment also raises the price of imports, and is thus likely to aggravate inflation. This effect can be limited by counter-inflationary austerity measures: tax increases, cuts in public spending, and the repression of workers' demands for higher pay. However, Latin American governments have often been unable to bring inflation under control, resulting in further REER increases and currency overvaluation. For example, after 1977 Mexican inflation continued at relatively high rates, and the peso had once again become considerably overvalued by the early 1980s, on the eve of the debt crisis.

Peronism   The political movement established by the Argentine populist leader Juan Perón.

populist   The term applied in Latin America to politicians who seek the support of a broad social coalition, including all classes except the landed elite, with a programme of ISI, welfare, and nationalist measures.

post-modernist   The term applied in this book to critics of neoliberalism who stress the value of small-scale, locally based popular collective action as a social and political strategy.

PRI   *Partido Revolucionario Institucional.* The name adopted in 1946 by the party that has dominated Mexican politics and government since the 1920s.

purchasing power parity   A statistical adjustment, taking account of differences between countries in living costs, sometimes made when calculating national output per head as a basis for international comparisons.

REER   Real effective exchange rate. See overvaluation.

sierra   Mountain, highland region.

SOE   State-owned enterprise.

statist   The term applied in this book to critics of neoliberalism who believe that the state can usefully play an active, interventionist role to

	promote economic development.
terms of trade	The average price of a country's exports relative to the average price of its imports. An increase of export prices relative to import prices represents an improvement in the terms of trade.
TNC	Transnational corporation. See MNC.
Washington consensus	The consensus established by the 1980s between the US government, the IMF, and the World Bank, favouring neoliberal economic policies.
World Bank	An international agency, based in Washington, D. C., providing medium- and long-term loans to developing countries.

Bibliography

Abel, C. and Lewis, C. M. (eds) (1993) *Welfare, Poverty and Development in Latin America*, London: Macmillan. Conference papers.

Balassa, B., Bueno, G., Kuczynski, P. and Simonsen, M. (1986) *Toward Renewed Economic Growth in Latin America*, Washington D. C.: Institute for International Economics. Uncompromising neoliberalism.

Banuri, T. (ed.) (1991) *Economic Liberalization: No Panacea; The Experiences of Latin America and Asia*, Oxford: Oxford University Press.

Bennett, D. C. and Sharpe, K. E. (1985) *Transnational Corporations Versus the State: The Political Economy of the Mexican Auto Industry*, Princeton: Princeton University Press. An exposition and critique of dependency theory, as it relates to the MNCs.

Bethell, L. (ed.) (1991) *The Cambridge History of Latin America*, vol. viii: *Latin America since 1930, Spanish South America*, Cambridge: Cambridge University Press.

—— (1994a) *The Cambridge History of Latin America*, vol. vi: *Latin America since 1930: Economy, Society and Politics, Part 1: Economy and Society*, Cambridge: Cambridge University Press.

—— (1994b) *The Cambridge History of Latin America*, vol. vi: *Latin America since 1930: Economy, Society and Politics, Part 2: Politics and Society*, Cambridge: Cambridge University Press.

Bethell, L. and Roxborough, I. (eds) (1992) *Latin America Between the Second World War and the Cold War: Crisis and Containment, 1944–48*, Cambridge: Cambridge University Press. Argues that deteriorating US–Soviet relations encouraged a swing back to authoritarian government in Latin America.

Branford, S. and Glock, O. (1985) *The Last Frontier: Fighting Over Land in the Amazon*, London: Zed Books.

Bulmer-Thomas, V. (1994) *The Economic History of Latin America Since Independence*, Cambridge: Cambridge University Press.

Carothers, T. (1991) *In the Name of Democracy: U.S. Policy Toward Latin America in the Reagan Years*, Berkeley, California: University of California Press. Written by a former State Department official.

Chant, S. (1991) *Women and Survival in Mexican Cities*, Manchester: Manchester University Press. Female employment trends during the 1980s.

Collins, J. and Lear, J. (1995) *Chile's Free-Market Miracle: A Second Look*, Oakland, California: The Institute for Food and Development Policy. A critique of Latin America's most celebrated neoliberal experiment. Contrast with Hojman (1993).

Cubitt, T. (1995), *Latin American Society*, 2nd edition, London: Longman. Hostile to neoliberalism.

Díaz-Briquets, S. (1983) *The Health Revolution in Cuba*, Austin, Texas: University of Texas Press. Puts the post-1959 Cuban mortality decline in longer-term perspective.

ECLAC (1992) *Education and Knowledge: Basic Pillars of Changing Production Patterns with Social Equity*, Santiago, Chile: Economic Commission for Latin America and the Caribbean. Education in Latin America, with wider comparisons.

Economist, The (1996) 10 February, 136.

—— (1997) 8 February, 146.

Evans, P. (1979) *Dependent Development: The Alliance of Multinational, State and Local Capital in Brazil*, Princeton, New Jersey: Princeton University Press. An adaptation of dependency theory.

FAO (1995) *FAO Yearbook: Production, 1994*, Rome: Food and Agriculture Organization.

Frieden, J. A. (1991) *Debt, Development, and Democracy: Modern Political Economy and Latin America, 1965–1985*, Princeton, New Jersey: Princeton University Press. The influence of domestic interest groups on economic policy.

Gereffi, G. and Wyman, D. L. (eds) (1990) *Manufacturing Miracles: Paths of Industrialization in Latin America and East Asia*, Princeton, New Jersey: Princeton University Press.

Gilbert, A. (1994) *The Latin American City*, London: Latin American Bureau.

Gleijeses, P. (1991) *Shattered Hope: The Guatemalan Revolution and the United States, 1944–1954*, Princeton, New Jersey: Princeton University Press. A remarkable monograph, vivid and detailed.

Goodman, D. and Hall, A. (eds) (1990) *The Future of Amazonia: Destruction or Sustainable Development?*, London: Macmillan. Includes historical material.

Goodman, D. and Redclift, M. (eds) (1991) *Environment and Development in Latin America*, Manchester: Manchester University Press. Argues that conventional economic strategies have proved bankrupt and unsustainable.

Green, D. (1991) *Faces of Latin America*, London: Latin America Bureau. An illustrated overview, 'left' in its assumptions.

—— (1995) *Silent Revolution: The Rise of Market Economics in Latin America*, London: Cassell. Highly critical of neoliberalism and its effects.

Haggard, S. (1990) *Pathways from the Periphery*, Ithaca, New York: Cornell University Press. Political economy of the East Asian 'Gang of Four', Mexico, and Brazil.

Halperin Donghi, T. (1993) *The Contemporary History of Latin America*, London: Macmillan. Mainly politics, with some economics.

Hewitt, T., Johnson, H. and Wield, D. (eds) (1992) *Industrialization and Development*, Oxford: Oxford University Press. Statist; compares Brazil and South Korea.

Hojman, D. (1993) *Chile: The Political Economy of Development and Democracy in the 1990s*, Pittsburgh: University of Pittsburgh Press.

Sympathetic to the neoliberal reforms. Compare with Collins and Lear (1995).

IMF (1996) *World Economic Outlook*, May issue, Washington, D. C.: International Monetary Fund. Reviews current trends from a neoliberal perspective, with Latin America's performance put in wider context.

de Janvry, A. (1981) *The Agrarian Question and Reformism in Latin America*, Baltimore, Maryland: The Johns Hopkins University Press. Why agrarian reform has failed to benefit the rural poor.

Jaquette, J. S. (ed.) (1989) *The Women's Movement in Latin America: Feminism and the Transition to Democracy*, Boston, Massachusetts and London: Unwin Hyman. Essays covering Brazil, Argentina, Uruguay, Peru, and Chile.

Keen, B. (1996) *A History of Latin America*, 5th edition, Boston, Massachusetts and Toronto: Houghton Mifflin. A survey text.

Lin, C. (1989) *Latin America vs East Asia: A Comparative Development Perspective*, Armonk, New York: M.E. Sharpe. Discriminating neoliberalism; concentrates on macroeconomic policy.

Lowenthal, A. F. (ed.) (1991) *Exporting Democracy: The United States and Latin America, Case Studies*, Baltimore, Maryland: The Johns Hopkins University Press.

Maddison, A. and associates (1992) *The Political Economy of Poverty, Equity, and Growth: Brazil and Mexico*, New York: Oxford University Press. Developments since 1945; a World Bank-sponsored study.

Martz, J. D. (ed.) (1988) *United States Policy in Latin America: A Quarter Century of Crisis and Challenge, 1961–1986*, Lincoln, Nebraska: University of Nebraska Press.

Morales, E. (1989) *Cocaine: White Gold Rush in Peru*, Tucson, Arizona: University of Arizona Press. Social background to the drugs trade.

Moran, T. H. (1974) *Multinational Corporations and the Politics of Dependence: Copper in Chile*, Princeton, New Jersey: Princeton University Press. The waning power of the US copper companies.

Morawetz, D. (1981) *Why the Emperor's New Clothes Are Not Made in Colombia: A Case Study in Latin American and East Asian Manufactured Exports*, New York: Oxford University Press. Neoliberal; a study sponsored by the World Bank.

Murray, D. L. (1994) *Cultivating Crisis: The Human Cost of Pesticides in Latin America*, Austin, Texas: University of Texas Press.

National Research Council (1993) *Sustainable Agriculture and the Environment in the Humid Tropics*, Washington, D. C.: National Academy Press. Overview, with chapters on Brazil and Mexico.

Radcliffe, S. A. and Westwood, S. (eds) (1993) *'Viva': Women and Popular Protest in Latin America*, London: Routledge. Case studies of NSMs in which women have taken a leading role.

Roberts, B. (1995) *The Making of Citizens: Cities of Peasants Revisited*, London: Arnold. Urban social mobility and stratification in Latin America.

Rouquié, A. (1987) *The Military and the State in Latin America*, Berkeley, California: University of California Press. Sophisticated analysis.

Shapiro, H. (1994) *Engines of Growth: The State and Transnational Auto Companies in Brazil*, Cambridge: Cambridge University Press.

Sheahan, J. (1987) *Patterns of Development in Latin America: Poverty, Repression, and Economic Strategy*, Princeton, New Jersey: Princeton University Press. Takes a reformist, 'middle of the road' course between dependency theory and neoliberalism.

Skidmore, T. E. and Smith, P. H. (1997) *Modern Latin America*, 4th edition, New York: Oxford University Press. National histories, with five other chapters drawing out general themes.

Smith, G. (1994) *The Last Years of the Monroe Doctrine, 1945–1993*, New York: Hill and Wang. A narrative, emphasizing the doctrine's strong influence on US attitudes to Latin America until the end of the cold war.

Stallings, B. (1987) *Banker to the Third World: U.S. Portfolio Investment in Latin America, 1900–1986*, Berkeley, California: University of California Press. Puts the 1980s debt crisis in longer-term perspective.

Tullis, LaMond (1995) *Unintended Consequences: Illegal Drugs and Drug Policies in Nine Countries*, Boulder, Colorado: Lynne Rienner. Covers Colombia, Peru, Bolivia, Mexico, and some Asian countries. Pessimistic views on the effectiveness of supply control policies.

Ward, P. M. (1990) *Mexico City: The Production and Reproduction of an Urban Environment*, London: Belhaven Press. Problems of Latin America's biggest conurbation.

Williamson, E. (1992) *The Penguin History of Latin America*, Harmondsworth: Penguin Books. A lucid overview.

Williamson, J. (ed.) (1990) *Latin American Adjustment: How Much Has Happened?*, Washington, D. C.: Institute for International Economics. Discussion of the Washington consensus and its influence. The editor coined the term.

World Bank (1978–96), *World Development Report*, New York: Oxford University Press. An annual review, neoliberal in its attitudes, with statistical appendices.

—— (1984b, 1984c) *World Tables*, 3rd edition, two volumes, Baltimore, Maryland: The Johns Hopkins University Press. A statistical compilation.

Wynia, G. W. (1990), *The Politics of Latin American Development*, 3rd edition, Cambridge: Cambridge University Press. The standard text on its subject.

Relevant academic journals include: *Bulletin of Latin American Research,* Oxford: Elsevier Science; *Hispanic American Historical Review*, Durham, North Carolina: Duke University Press; *Journal of Latin American Studies*, Cambridge: Cambridge University Press; *Latin American Research Review*, Albuquerque, New Mexico: University of New Mexico Press. *The Handbook of Latin American Studies*, Austin, Texas: Texas University Press, provides an annual bibliographical update. Current developments may be followed through the annual ECLAC, *Economic Survey of Latin America and the Caribbean*, Santiago: United Nations; *The Economist*, London: The Economist Newspaper Ltd, strongly neoliberal; and *Latin America Weekly Report*, London: Latin American Newsletters. S. Collier and T. Skidmore, (eds), *The Cambridge Encyclopaedia of Latin America and the Caribbea*n, 2nd edition, Cambridge: Cambridge University Press, 1992, is a useful reference work.

Index